More Praise for Hope Rising

"As you immerse yourself in this modern-day miracle, believe that the same God will enable you to achieve great things to serve the needs of others. Dream big with God!"

—**Dr. LaDonna Osborn**, Osborn Ministries
International

"In Hope Rising, Joyce Strong shows how empty hands and poverty can open the door to the greatest God has for us. She tells the story of the hope, the glory, the pain, the thrill, the discouragement and the ultimate 'win' when God's people let go of self-reliance, trust him and obey."

—**Kathy Chiero**, Host of The Sitting Room
radio show, Columbus, OH

"Hope Rising will inspire you to put your faith into action and see what God will do. Use this book to light a fire in your own circle of influence. God is looking for world changers!"

—**Cindy Schmidt**, Missions Director, New
New Life Church, Gahanna, OH

"The stirring story of Blessings Hope reminds me of the First Century Christians—living by faith, patiently battling tribulations and spiritual attacks, standing firm in their confidence in God and anchored in Jesus Christ. Hope Rising will inspire and encourage you in your own walk of faith."

—**Linda J. White**, Award-winning author
of Seeds of Evidence

Hope
Rising

Hope
Rising

*The True Story of a Place in Kenya Where
God Dreams and Miracles Happen!*

JOYCE STRONG,

WITH PASTOR SAMUEL WAFULA AND FRIENDS

XULON PRESS

Xulon Press
2301 Lucien Way #415
Maitland, FL 32751
407.339.4217
www.xulonpress.com

Printed in the United States of America.

ISBN-13: 9781545602812

Table of Contents

Dedication

*H*ope Rising is dedicated to the memory of a sweet Blessings Hope student, Mercy Musau, who was about to enter her last year of high school. Mercy went to be with Jesus after her tragic death on December 4, 2016, in Birunda Village, Kenya, where she had gone on semester break to help her mother. All who knew her and wept at her passing will rejoice with her in heaven someday.

Acknowledgements

*I*t is my great joy to introduce Pastor Samuel Wafula, Director of Blessings Hope Educational Centre and "Dreamer Extraordinaire"; his father Bishop Michael Wafula who laid a powerful faith and service foundation in Samuel; the gifted and wise Blessings Hope Educational Centre teachers and the delightful, wholehearted students whom they instruct, love and mentor. I would like to express my deep respect for Pastor Samuel's leadership team and the staff who make everything flow seamlessly on the farm and at the polytechnic, as well as those who carry the day to-day responsibilities at the Centre.

God bless you all!

In Appreciation

I am deeply grateful for my husband Jim who not only supports and encourages me as I minister wherever in the world God calls me, but prays and sacrifices with me for the success of Blessings Hope Educational Centre. I thank my son Scott and daughter Julie for their technical counsel in the shaping of this book.

My sincere thanks go out to my ministry buddy Carol Middendorf, whom God brought alongside me at exactly the right time to be a channel of God's blessing to the school and to the widows at Blessings Hope. May she and her husband Don be blessed beyond measure for their generosity and passion for what matters to God.

Special thanks go out to all the donors in the U.S. and Russia who have also fallen in love with the dear children and widows at Blessings Hope and, although never having set eyes on them, have contributed so generously to give them hope. For you who sponsor orphans, teachers and widows monthly, know that your consistent, cumulative deposit into their lives makes all the difference in the world to them and to the success of Blessings Hope! And for you who give often at great sacrifice whenever there is a crisis of need, you continually humble and bless me by your example.

Foundational to all these contributors are those friends who have supported Joyce Strong Ministries monthly from the very beginning nearly 20 years ago. You have been quiet, faithful warriors of God, praying and giving, making possible every ministry trip I have made into Russia, England, India, Uganda and Kenya. Thank you for standing with me!

I also owe a tremendous debt of gratitude to Beth Mutua, my personal friend and talented translator of this and several other of my books from English into Kiswahili. Her excellent translations have made the books accessible to thousands upon thousands of men and women who would otherwise not benefit from them. I praise God for her and all she contributes to the Body of Christ as not only a translator and interpreter, but a teacher and minister of the Gospel.

Most of all, we acknowledge God as the "Holy Dream Giver," life restorer and healer who alone has authored the call that has gripped our hearts and lives. We praise him and give him all the glory for the miracles that have sustained and uplifted us all. He has done marvelous things!

Note to Readers

This book is a collaborative effort. While I, Joyce, am the primary author of this book, you will also hear from Pastor Samuel, Carol Middendorf, the Blessings Hope teachers and, of course, the students. Their names will be in the headings of any sections in which their voices join the narrative.

It has been quite an adventure to draw all our thoughts into one cohesive message while on opposite sides of the world! I am in awe of how the Holy Spirit has orchestrated our lives and times so that we could make the journey joyfully and together.

Preface

I am convinced that God's dreams for us were in his heart before we were born, perhaps even before time began. He knew all that would happen on this earth as a result of sin. He knew there would be wars and hatred, fatherless children, lonely widows and broken hearts.

And so he dreamed "holy dreams" that would fill our hearts with hope and challenge us to act. He dreamed of how his Son would pay the price for our sins and free us from the grip of darkness, reuniting us with himself. He also dreamed that we would hear the same cries for healing and deliverance that he hears and move to be his agents of change. His dreams have always revealed the very substance of his heart—his love and purposes for us all.

Such dreams never surprise God, but they surely surprise us—especially the big ones. Dreams that are a natural outgrowth of our interests and abilities are "no brainers." But those that he whispers into our hearts at the most unlikely of times and which require us to do the impossible—those which we don't think "fit" us at all—shock us to our core. We are never ready for them.

But God is.

Prologue

by Pastor Samuel Wafula

Director of Blessings Hope Educational Centre, Kitale, Kenya

*W*hat a great pleasure and blessing to assure you that God answers prayers and fulfills visions and dreams! I hope you will agree with me as you read our book.

First, I would like to tell you how and why Joyce Strong has become a spiritual mother, a mum, to me and to Blessings Hope.

Before I met our beloved Mum Joyce Strong, my ministry was weaving in many directions. There was nobody I could share with or seek advice from because everyone was busy working for the establishment of their own families and ministries. Due to this, I had a hard time.

Here in Kenya we have a saying that behind every successful man, there is a woman. So I did research to find the secret behind well-established and growing ministries. What I discovered was that they had strong mentors behind them. After knowing the secret, I went on my knees and asked God to connect me with someone who has the seal of God and a mentoring heart. I tried to approach many servants of God across the country and even beyond our continent, but none responded positively.

But I kept praying. I had a vision that one of these fine days, God would fulfill my desire. After some years of prayers, God connected me with a very wonderful and beautiful mum, Joyce Strong. After I contacted her through email, I started reading her books which she sent to me through her friends from the States. Then my lifestyle started to change, as well as my family and the ministry. Many people said that they were seeing a great change in my life and the ministry and asked, "What is behind all this?"

I told them that God had connected me with someone whose books I was reading. They kept saying, "That's the right person for you to work and move together with!" I too realized that she was the right person to ask for mentorship because everyone was seeing the fruits in my life. According to the book of *Luke 6:43-45, Jesus said that a good tree is known by its fruits...*

My agape love for our beloved Mum Joyce Strong continued to grow day after day, and since my life was being inspired by her books, I also shared them with the body of Christ here in Kenya. God spoke in mighty ways to whoever was reading the books. Everyone was so encouraged and blessed with great insights that were revelations to us! I was so encouraged that I wanted to meet her personally.

So I started another journey of prayer for God to make a way so that one of these fine days I might meet her, shake her hand and even have fellowship with her. I am blessed to let you know again that God answered my prayers and opened a way for us to meet. In fact our meeting was miraculous. In August of 2011, around 4:00 pm, I came across a short email from Mum Joyce telling me that she was on her way to the airport to fly to our neighboring country, Uganda, to speak at a Women's Leadership Seminar followed by a Women's Conference, and suggesting that we meet there.

I was very happy. Although my schedule was full, I dismissed everything else and started making arrangements to go. I called all of my friends and shared with them the great news and asked them to pray with me for travel mercies. Everyone was very happy and ready to partner with me in prayers for the success of the trip. After two days, I started my journey to Kampala, Uganda. Despite a lot of obstacles, God made a way and I arrived very well and was warmly accepted by Pastor Peter Kasirivu and his wife Irene, my hosts. It was very late—around midnight—but they gave me good care.

Although I was very tired after traveling more than 18 hours, my heart was anxious to meet our beloved mum. Even before the first cock crowed, I was already up thanking God for the beautiful day. I prepared very early and called Pastor Peter, who then took me to the venue. In fact I was the first person on the grounds! Later I was joined by the church choir. They asked me several questions. For instance, "Why are you here since the conference is for women?" I told them that although the conference was for women, in my spirit I was feeling that there would be a word for me too.

After a few hours of worship, I saw Mum Joyce being escorted to church. It was like "daytime dreaming," for in my heart I felt that God was answering my prayers. I attended the entire Leadership Seminar until it was time for the Women's Conference. Then I was able to greet her and shake her hand. I was joined by a great friend of mine, Bishop Moses from Uganda, and it was surely a new day for me. I don't know how to express my joy. I went on to the Women's Conference but had to leave at the break. I didn't even wait until I reached home to make phone calls, sharing testimonies with my family members and friends of all that had happened. It was on that day in Uganda that my connection with Mum Joyce truly grew in strength.

Because of the wonderful ministry she did in Uganda, I asked her to come to Kenya the following year since many were in much need of her ministry of healing and intimacy with God. She told me that we could pray and see what God would do. By the very next year, God made a way, and she was able to fly to Kenya. Surely God is faithful and always ready to answer prayer and fulfill our visions and dreams.

Part One

WHEN GOD DREAMS

Chapter One

An African Dreamer

In his heart a man plans his course, but the LORD
determines his steps. Proverbs 16:9

Joyce:

*I*t was a hot, breezy, August day in Kampala, Uganda. I was speaking at a Women's Leadership Seminar for Gaba Community Church. The year was 2011.

A tall, slender young man in a peach-colored suit entered the classroom and slipped into a seat. It seemed not to matter to him that he was the only male in a room that was filling quickly with vibrant women leaders of all ages. Throughout the sessions, he was silently engaged, taking notes and listening intently. At the close of the seminar, he quietly stepped outside the classroom and waited patiently for someone as I chatted with the women while they were given copies of *Leading with Passion and Grace,* one of my books on leadership.

As I left the building, the young man in the peach-colored suit stepped forward to introduce himself as Pastor Samuel Wafula, founder of Gospel Outreach Evangelism Ministries, Kenya.

Ah, so this is Pastor Samuel, the earnest young man whom I had hoped to meet. A year earlier, after being contacted by him via email, I had asked friends to visit him with some of my books and check out his ministry. I had wanted to know about the integrity and spirit of his ministry in particular. They came back with this assessment: "Samuel is very poor, but he is the 'real deal.' It's incredible what he is doing with practically nothing!"

I discovered that Samuel is a man of few words: intense, thoughtful and humble yet with the quiet dignity that rests on someone whose vision comes from a pure heart and a true call to preach the Gospel. I was very impressed.

During the course of our conversation, we were joined by another young man of like passion, Pastor Moses Mukembo. They were good friends who often ministered together, partners in Christ across the border they share between Kenya and Uganda.

In the few minutes available before the Women's Conference would begin, Samuel invited me to come back to Africa the next year to speak at a Leadership Conference at his father's ministry in Kiminini, Kenya. I agreed to pray about it.

Pastor Samuel, outside the classroom

I did indeed return to Africa in the spring of the following year to speak at a Women's Conference and Leaders' Conference at his father's ministry site. My friend Linda Lewis from Columbus, OH, traveled with me. After we arrived at the ministry, I was surprised to see a lovely banner hanging behind the podium expressing the partnership of Joyce Strong Ministries and Samuel's ministry, Gospel Outreach Evangelism Ministry, as hosts of the event. But it felt right.

Little did I know that before the end of our time together, God would set in motion an outrageous "holy dream" that would stretch my heart at least ten sizes and teach me what really matters to *him*.

On the last day of the Leaders' Conference, Samuel announced that we would be stopping first at a little school building on rented land. There were some special children he wanted me to meet and pray for who had experienced terrible losses and pain during post-election violence.

You see, much of Africa is still very tribal. The people's roots are part of who they are, and for many election cycles since Kenya gained its independence from Great Britain in 1960, uprisings of one tribe against another have been common. Hence, the weakest—the children—end up hiding in the bush or simply running for their lives when their parents are killed and their homes and villages destroyed.

But Samuel and others with God's heart of compassion have a way of finding these terrified, hungry children and taking them in. That's how many children's homes and orphanages have begun in Africa. Those sanctuaries that are able soon attempt to educate the children, knowing that an education will be crucial in building a new future and reversing the trend of violence and poverty that can so easily devastate any country.

Samuel:

God brought the children to us in different ways. Most of the ones with whom we started and whom Mum Joyce would meet that morning in 2012, I encountered as I was conducting outreach missions to the people of Birunda Village. God had put it into our hearts just to be vessels of hope and healing for these wounded people. A majority of them had been hurt deeply during the 1990 tribal clashes as well as during 2007 post-election violence. Much of our time was spent visiting them in their rental places, just praying with them and encouraging them in their troubles.

During our regular visitations, we realized that most of the children we saw on the streets were not attending any schools. They were just roaming around and even being hired out as day laborers. We wanted to know more about why they were not attending the schools. According to the research we did and the interviews we had with the people, we discovered that most of the children had lost their parents, and their guardians were not able to finance their studies due to poor income.

All of this took me back to a heartbreaking encounter I had had as a young boy trying to stay in school myself. Here is the story:

At 9:00 a.m. on a Monday morning in 1994, while I was in Class Three (third grade), a school official came into our classroom with a list of the names of more than three hundred children who had not paid their school fees. At least ten children from my class were on that list and were sent back home to return with the fees. I was among them.

This happened in the middle of my favorite lesson, and I had to immediately leave. After I had traveled a few meters from school, I came across a young boy who was from my school and almost my age. He was shedding many tears, and his heart was full of pain. I was drawn to him. I wanted to know what had happened to him.

I humbly asked him, "My brother, why are you crying, and why is your heart so full of pain?"

He told me, "I wish my parents could be alive, then I would not be always on my way home to bring back school fees. It's my desire to learn, but because of my situation and the hard life we are undergoing, it seems that I am going to miss accomplishing the desire of my heart. I am seeing my dreams going to the grave."

This really shocked my heart and I wanted to know more. "What happened to your parents?" I asked.

He answered sadly, "They were killed during 1990-1992 tribalism clashes. I was left with my younger brother and sister as well as my grandmother who is 91 years old. She is a widow and can't do anything to support us or to pay my school fees."

I then asked how they are surviving, and he told me that they always depend on good Samaritans. But most of the time he is the breadwinner of the family. He explained, "If a good Samaritan cannot help with our meals, I go and find casual work to do so that I can buy something for them to eat."

I kept asking him more questions, including how often he attended the school. He told me that mostly it was just two days per week instead of five days. While he was sharing his story with me, I could see that he was feeling more sadness and pain.

He told me, "This could be the end of going back to school because I must now focus on finding some way to take care of my old grandmother as well as my younger brother and sister." And he cried again.

Surely, this really broke my heart, and my eyes began to be opened to the tragedy that many children experience.

I too was born in a very poor family where we could not know the difference between breakfast or lunch, for it was just a slice of ugali and some vegetables which were boiled, sometimes without salt. However, unlike my schoolmate, I had parents and could experience their love. But life was very difficult for us. They could not provide for us many of our basic needs. If you could visit us and see where we were sleeping, then you would cry, because we had only old sacks to cover ourselves which did not keep us warm when it was very cold.

Also, the school fees were a big challenge. My parents could not pay for me or my brothers, sisters or the orphans who were under their care. My studies were really affected because I had to leave school to find casual work just to pay for my school fees as well as for my dear ones. Sometimes when I was sent home to go and bring back the school fees—because I understood our circumstances—I did not bother to go home. I simply went out to find some way to raise the cash.

So when I heard the hard and painful story of the young boy, a burden in my heart grew for him and others like him. I then made a covenant with God. If God would bless me one day and take me out of this hardship, then I would open a school and home to take care of orphans and the needy so that they will not have to bury their vision and dreams.

Many years later, as I met the orphaned children of Birunda, God stirred up that covenant within me. I saw that he had blessed me and prepared me to prevent the loss of hopes and dreams among the very children we were meeting.

So I began dreaming of setting up a school. I posted the information to my team members, and we started to pray for God to give us direction. After some time, God revealed to me where to start. Again I outlined it all to the team, and we took a step and shared with the community the importance of education. We cast the vision, and they were so happy for it! They embraced the vision, followed the guidelines, and that's how they brought these children to us. We started renting a small building in a field, and school began. The teachers were volunteers. Glory to God!

Board members and guardians outside this tiny school

Joyce:

I didn't know Samuel's story yet, and on that May morning in 2012, I had no desire to see orphans no matter how gripping their stories. I feared that my heart would be devastated and I would be helpless to do anything for them. At that point, I'd just rather not feel anything. So I would steel myself against their sadness and pray for them, and then I would go on to the conference, finish teaching and go home.

Chapter Two

The Dream Seed is Sown

I am the LORD your God, who teaches you what is best for you,
who directs you in the way you should go. Isaiah 48:17b

Joyce:

I' ll never forget pulling into the open field where the children were waiting for us. It was a clear, beautiful day that brought the distant mountains close. Morning dew still clung to the grass making my bare feet slide in my sandals. To the right stood a small brick and cement building partitioned into two tiny rooms in which were simple wooden benches. Blackboards leaned against the cement front walls. The children waited quietly outside in a little group in front of a brick wall a short distance away that seemed to have once been part of a building, but which now stood alone.

At first, the children didn't smile. Most of them looked a bit apprehensive as they sized up this strange-looking, white-haired *mzungu* (white woman) who had suddenly appeared with Pastor Samuel. A few wore passed-down green school uniforms that they had been given perhaps by their guardians.

One little girl with the saddest face and a furrowed brow wore a dusty sweater with a teddy bear embroidered on the front—a sweater that had seen better days long ago. The strap of an old purse crossed her little body, the bag itself hanging down to her knees. I wished I could take her home with me. As I searched that small face, I could only imagine what life had been like for her before being rescued by strangers and given hope by Samuel and his team.

My "teddy bear orphan"

When one of the smiling teachers called for everyone's attention, all the children turned toward her with relief, and reciprocal smiles began to appear. I don't know what she said to them, but they responded in a way that made me believe that they would follow that sweet lady anywhere!

Since their language is Kiswahili, they would likely understand nothing of what I would say to them. I tried an encouraging sentence or two, but when I saw no response, I decided to keep it simple. Simplicity would also help keep me from getting emotionally involved. My heart wouldn't be able to take it. While fighting back the tears, I prayed for them—for their healing, salvation, care and comfort—and for the attentive volunteers who so obviously loved the children.

Responding to their sweet teacher

I made it through the brief visit and thanked the adults for what they were doing. Then Samuel motioned that we needed to continue on to the conference. Gratefully, I walked quickly back to his Jeep and climbed in, closing off the scene I had left behind in the field.

Praying for them

Speaking later that day; Bishop Michael Wafula, Samuel's father, interpreting

That evening, after the conference ended and I was packing to leave Kenya, I thought I had emotionally and mentally stayed above it all reasonably well. Early the next morning, Samuel saw Linda and me off at the primitive air station outside Kitale. A 12-seat prop plane made the two-hour flight to the international airport in Nairobi where we boarded a Delta flight for Amsterdam, and then on to the States. With a sigh of relief, I sank into my window seat and closed my eyes.

But somewhere over the Atlantic, God's voice pierced my heart. "They need their own land," he said clearly.

"So what can *I* do about it?" I whispered. When he simply repeated, "They need their own land," I took him seriously.

"Okay," I sighed. "I'll find out how much an acre costs. But Jim and I have only a few thousand in savings, and I'm not going to hit on all my friends for it!" He didn't respond. However, a plan began to form in my mind in spite of my resistance.

"Lord, if you will give me the names of four people who together can give enough to buy that land, I'll write to them and tell them what you have said. I will describe the situation and the need and ask them to pray. If you want them to give money, *you'll* have to tell them to do it."

There, the onus was back on God. If this dream was truly from him, he would bring it to pass.

He gave me the names in a matter of a few minutes.

When I got home, I emailed Samuel and asked him what the land would cost. After talking to the owner of a good piece of land with room for expansion, he wrote back that it would cost $7,000. My husband Jim and I donated the first $1,000, and I sent the letters. In four days, the remaining $6,000 came in the mail. Throughout this time, Samuel and his church had been on their knees.

And so began the stretching of my heart as God began a relentless realignment of my passion to match his own.

Samuel:

As we continued to serve God faithfully in this great ministry in that little building, we realized more and more that our space was very small, with many children having to sit close together on the floor. We also realized that we were risking our lives and the lives of these children by not following the constitutional rules of education in our land of Kenya.

My faith entered a big trial. Discouragement started to flow my way, but I kept my faith and trust in the Lord God, knowing that he will supply everything according to his riches.

One night as I was just resting in my sitting room in our rental house, I was thanking God in my heart for the children and the land that I didn't know how we could buy. I believed that he was about to supply the land without my having any clue where I would get the funds.

While in that mood, a phone call came from a number I didn't recognize. I received the phone call and realized that it was Mum Joyce who was calling, full of good news! She asked me how much it would cost to buy one acre of land. My heart began to fill with joy! Since I was not sure exactly how much it would be, I told her that I would get back to her later with a confirmation.

In two days' time, I was able to know the price and get back to her. Within a few more days, she sent the funds for our first acre of land. Wow, what a mighty and marvelous God we are serving!

Surely God never gives us dreams without providing for them. I guess it was right then that the partnership between Blessings Hope and Joyce Strong Ministries began.

Joyce:

As soon as the donations had arrived and I had wired the money for the land to Samuel, God spoke again:

The orphans need a home. They also need a school building for that land.

I had no idea how we would do all this, but with a lump in my throat and my heart pounding, I wrote to Samuel and asked him to have an architect draw up plans for the buildings that would be necessary to establish the orphans' home and the school. I advised him to think ahead, to plan for the future even as we began building. He enlisted an architect who sketched beautiful, but very practical plans. He also hired an engineer whom he trusted to oversee the work.

Here's where God shocked me with his sovereignty.

You see, I have a very special friend named Carol Middendorf. She and I had served together in the Women's Ministry in New Life Church in Gahanna, OH, for several years, and she had traveled with me to Russia, Uganda and Kenya in the past. We have different spiritual gifts, but the same heart. Every Tuesday we meet at a cafe to encourage each other in Christ, laugh, cry, pray and be gentle accountability partners.

When I returned from Kenya in 2012 all excited about what God had begun by speaking to me while flying over the Atlantic on my way home, I shared it with her. She simply said, "Let's pray about it."

Later, I was awestruck by the unique role God had been preparing her to play in the dream and how God had planned the intersecting of our lives for the sake of orphans and widows on the other side of the world.

Carol:

It's amazing to me that God had known that someday Joyce and I would meet and become friends. He had also known long ago that one day my own parents' generosity would play a major role in blessing children far away.

My parents were not wealthy people; my father had an insurance business in a small city in Ohio. But once when his business was faltering, he prayed and asked God to bless his business so that he could bless others. God answered that prayer with great blessing, and my father made good on his own promise.

Following my mother's death in 2002, my father established a college scholarship fund in her honor for high school seniors who were members of our church. A few scholarships had been given prior to and after my father's death in 2005, but I felt that God had **more** planned for the money. At the time that Joyce told me about Kenya and Pastor Samuel, I had already (with the agreement of other family members) used some of it to help build a school in Uganda through our church. So I spoke again with my brothers, and we prayed about it. We agreed that my parents would be honored to know that another Christian school and orphanage would be built using these funds.

The funny thing is that Joyce hadn't known that I was the administrator of that fund, and it had never crossed her mind that I could help in such a way. She was just asking for prayer!

The rest is history: Two orphans' houses, two widows' houses and two classroom buildings are now in full use at Blessings Hope because of God's blessing upon my dad and my dad's love of helping others succeed. Over these past few years, my husband Don and I, as well as my entire family, have had the joy of helping Blessings Hope Educational Centre in many ways.

Chapter Three

Obedience and Fellow Dreamers

Two are better than one, because they have a good return
for their work: If one falls down, his friend can help him up.

Ecclesiastes 4:9

Joyce:

reams are multi-layered. Those who dare dream find themselves in the *middle* of each adventure, alongside others who have also been prepared in other times and seasons to be partners in the dream. Carol was one of those prepared to partner with me even though I had not known it.

However, back when God originally planted his dream of Blessings Hope in my heart in that plane high above the Atlantic Ocean in 2012, I had *felt* alone. To my husband Jim, as kind as he was, it would sound like a fantasy. All our personal resources were going toward paying off our home mortgage in the few years we still had before turning 75! We had no secret cache for such a dream.

When I shared with him all that had happened in Kenya, what I described was literally a world away from what he could imagine, never having been there. It was one thing to stand with me as I traveled to other lands with the message of healing and wholeness in Jesus Christ, but it was quite another thing when I brought the needs and tears of suffering children home with me.

But Jim knew that hearing from God was real and trustworthy. In 1992, when we were living in Bradenton, Florida, Jim had been out of work for six months. He had interviewed for several positions, including Church Business Administrator at a large church in Sarasota, but nothing had materialized. Since our savings were quickly disappearing and occasional temporary jobs did not provide much income, Jim urged me to apply for a teaching position with a local Christian school. It was not the direction I preferred, but Jim's thinking was that at least *one* of us should find a full-time job! Following an interview with the school's principal, I was offered the job. All I needed to do was to come in the following Monday to sign the contract.

That Sunday morning as we sat quietly in church listening to the pastor's sermon, God spoke to Jim. God told him three things: that I should turn down the teaching contract; he should be responsible for our income; and I should be free to follow my heart. After church, Jim looked pale and somewhat shaken as he shared with me what God had spoken into his heart. It was wonderful news for me that I could turn down the teaching job and seek *God's* plan for my life, but could I trust that Jim truly had heard from God and refuse the job when we needed income so badly?

We spent the rest of the morning and much of the afternoon walking back and forth on the white sands of Coquina Beach on the Gulf of Mexico, brainstorming as to what "follow my heart" might actually look like. Out of that time together came the inspiration for writing my first book, *Lambs on the Ledge: Seeing and Avoiding Danger in Spiritual Leadership.*

I had never seriously considered being an author, although my students at both Teen Challenge Training Center in PA, and others later at Bible Teachers' Institute in VA, had urged me to write a book containing what I was teaching them so that it could reach more people. But I just laughed about it at the time. I loved the interaction that classroom teaching afforded and had no interest in trying to sit still long enough to write a book!

But God was changing everything.

Monday came quickly enough, and I had to commit to believing Jim's revelation and call the school to turn down their offer. But I couldn't quite do it. When Tuesday came I knew I *must* stake our financial future on believing that Jim really *did* hear from God and be obedient. I called the school and turned down the contract. It felt like putting a knife through our checkbook, but I stepped out in faith in God and trusted what he had spoken to Jim. The rest of the day was quiet and uneventful for us both except for a nagging fear that we'd committed financial suicide!

However, the very next day Jim received a telephone call from the head of the Personnel Committee at the church in Sarasota, FL, where he had applied months earlier, offering him the Church Business Administrator position and saying he could start immediately! Between Sunday morning and Wednesday, God had launched Jim into a new career and ministry in the church, and had effected a complete change of ministry direction for me.

The publication of *Lambs on the Ledge* opened up exciting adventures as an author and speaker with opportunities to encourage leaders in the U.S. and abroad. I probably would never have met

Samuel or heard from God in a plane over the Atlantic in 2012 if I hadn't believed God's word to Jim and turned down that teaching job. *Obedience is always key to the next move of God!*

So Jim already firmly believed that God *does* speak directly to us, but he had many good and reasonable questions: Could we trust Samuel? What would be required? When would it end?

While I tried to answer these, the only one that really mattered surfaced: Was this truly *God's* dream and not just mine?

Over time, God confirmed that the dream had been in *his* heart from the beginning, and that he had indeed chosen my tiny ministry to partner with Pastor Samuel on behalf of the helpless. Many have been the miracles of answered prayer and times of encouragement and direction as I have met with God in solitude in the woods near our home. Many have been the tears as he confirmed his will not only in the woods, but through people who had "words from the Lord" for me. Many have been the mysterious ways God has had of bringing someone into the dream to solve a problem that was confounding us. All of this has convinced us both of the authenticity of the dream and our role in it.

Before partnering with Pastor Samuel and the children, my supporters had been accustomed to my raising funds for book translations and a couple of ministry trips a year to Russia, India, England or East Africa. However, I had feared that they would quite reasonably desert me as the needs mounted that are inevitable when building an orphanage and school and caring for what would quickly become well over 100 children. But they stayed the course, and more have joined us!

You see, God has captured their hearts for something greater than themselves. They continue to respond to a vast array of appeals with prayer and financial gifts as the Holy Spirit prompts them *even though most of them have never personally seen the children or the ministry there*. Their trust and sacrifice are amazing!

This is the pattern God has established: I learn of a need. If I sense God speaking to my heart about it, Jim and I pray about it and then give what we can. Then I share the need with friends and family members and ask them to pray. The vision captures the hearts of an army of "holy dreamers"—men and women in the U.S. and beyond whose hearts have been prepared and are ready to respond unselfishly with joy again and again.

Ever since God first spoke, their gifts have arrived in the nick of time—for beds, mattresses, food, playground equipment, curriculum, uniforms, a tractor and trailer, cows, goats, chickens, generators, more land to cultivate for food, electricity, Samuel's home, a roof for the new church, a motorcycle, a van, shoes, clothes, three businesses, insurance, hospital bills, mosquito netting, and high school and college tuition. There is never extra money, but always just enough. Meanwhile, Samuel and the church move mountains to meet a great many other needs every single day.

I know that Samuel would agree with me that there are times when all we can do is cry out to the Lord when the dream seems to be a fool's errand. However, sooner or later, God always answers. And we know that neither God nor we are fools. While we wait, he takes our faith deeper than we ever imagined possible.

25

Chapter Four

The Dream Takes Shape

Have I not commanded you? Be strong and courageous. Do not be terrified; do not be discouraged, for the LORD your God will be with you wherever you go. Joshua 1:9

Samuel:

After purchasing the land, we were in need of classrooms and dormitories for the children. We praise God since he is so faithful. Always he knows our needs even before we pray! So as we kept our eyes on Jesus Christ of Nazareth for provision, he provided the funds through Mum Joyce's dear friend Carol and her family's scholarship fund.

Immediately we started the construction. This generous contribution enlightened the community and revealed the great love which God has for them. In addition, apart from serving the children, construction created employment for the community. This contributed very highly to the growth of our economy in this region.

Joyce:

Laying the foundation of the first classroom building and the first orphans' house began in the summer of 2012. I'll never forget seeing the pictures of the workers making bricks out of the red earth, working in mud up to their ankles, pant legs rolled up, backs bent all day, and rows and rows of straw-covered bricks drying in the sun.

Workers making bricks

Construction begins

Pits were dug and brick outhouses were built over them. A lovely gazebo—round, built with brick up four feet and a metal roof above supported by posts—arose between the classroom and the cook house. How I loved standing in the shade of that gazebo when I returned in the fall of 2013! The breeze cooled more gently than air-conditioning ever could. And the view! From the gazebo westward could be seen Mt. Elgon stretching from north to south. It is into these mountains that Samuel and his gospel outreach team would often go to minister in remote villages, taking Jesus' love and his plan of salvation and healing with them every time.

On the other side of the temporary cookhouse of mud and sticks rose a truly lovely house in which the children would live. The design was so pleasing! Samuel had indeed chosen a good architect.

Of course, as the buildings took shape, Blessings Hope needed bunk beds, mattresses, bedding, school desks and books, teachers' desks and curriculum and teachers. When I shared the dream with my supporters in the U.S. and Europe, people willingly prayed and joyously gave so quickly that everything came together in record time—even the rest of the uniforms required for school!

First classroom building

First orphans' house

Samuel:

Always we needed to keep in our minds that even in good things, there will be challenges. After the construction and everything, new government rules were implemented and the school curriculum was changed. It was a big challenge since the time we were given in which we had to comply was very short. But we handed this care to God. I also shared with our Mum Joyce about the situation without expecting something from her. She and others had already done so much!

Joyce:

The Kenyan school year begins in January and runs into November. The goal was for the school to open in January 2013. The plan was to continue using volunteer teachers and whatever materials were at hand.

Just before opening day, the first shock wave from the government hit. At the last minute, new laws were passed that every school in Kenya had to use government-approved curriculum and government-certified teachers. This is actually a very good standard to have, but it was, on its surface, devastating to the school. Everything had to be suspended. School could not open. The sorrow in Samuel's emails was palpable.

So we prayed on both sides of the Atlantic: "God! Provide for the dream!"

The need that God laid upon me was for the curriculum. But this was after fundraising for many months for everything else they had needed. When I got the news, I bottomed out. I had a cold and was exhausted emotionally from all the fundraising to get this far.

I couldn't sleep that night. I was angry and ready to throw in the towel.

"God, is this really *your* dream? Am I really the person you want to dream with you for Blessings Hope?" I cried into my hands while bent over the kitchen table. "I really just want to quit and lead a simple life! I can't keep doing this!" Feeling incredibly sorry for myself, I continued my complaint: "How can I ask my friends to pray and seek God again for funding? Haven't we done enough?

"If this is really you, Lord, speak to me! Say *something* to encourage me!" I begged.

I listened intently for his voice. Nothing. Silence. I dragged myself up to bed to get a little sleep before dawn.

The next morning, I went to a coffee shop two miles from our home to spend quiet time with God. I took a seat by the large windows that look out upon the soothing landscaping that rings the cafe and separates it from the sidewalk leading to the parking lot. My heart grew still. Then I turned to read my Bible.

Two teachers from the New Albany high school, who were walking by the window on their way from the parking lot, caught my attention. One of the teachers glanced at me for just a second before heading toward the entrance. I forgot about them and returned to reading.

A few minutes later, a man's voice cut through my concentration.

"Excuse me, I don't know you but as I passed the window, God spoke to me. He said, "I have a message for you to give to that woman." He hesitated for a moment to make sure I didn't think he was crazy, then ventured, "May I tell you what he said?"

"Yes, please!" I quickly responded. "I really *need* to hear from him this morning!"

Smiling with relief and quite convinced I wouldn't call the police, the teacher repeated what God had said, "Tell her that I love her."

Tears welled up in my eyes. It was all I had needed to hear from God! If he loved me, I knew everything would be all right. I could trust him and I could trust the dream. Suddenly I knew that he would open hearts to give the money needed to purchase the curriculum. I had nothing to worry about. In fact, a 10-ton weight fell from my shoulders.

I couldn't wait to get home and share the need with the people who were coming to mind. Each one gave, and within two days, all $2,000 had arrived!

The way God supplied five certified teachers was even more amazing. Because many schools had been required to close for lack of the curriculum, there were some certified teachers who were unemployed. Lo and behold, one by one, five very fine teachers appeared at Blessings Hope curious about jobs and ready to go to work! They had heard of "the dream" and wanted to be part of it. This all happened within just a week after the school had been closed.

With incredible joy, Blessings Hope Educational Centre officially opened by mid-January, 2013!

Pastor Samuel is very strategic and farsighted. His dreams not only have huge substance, they have legs! He always knows that he must walk out the ramifications of his dreams. They will require action and preparation on his part. And so he takes action that will cause each dream to have a superior outcome.

From the beginning, he knew that more land would be needed—land that could produce much of the food they would need to feed all the children and staff. Joyce Strong Ministries could raise the funds to buy the land, but he would need to learn how to farm in a way that used a few acres to the best advantage and produced an abundance of healthful food. The land could not simply be planted in the same crop year after year as is common in Africa, but must be rotated and nurtured to produce what would be needed.

Samuel heard about a Christian organization, Farming God's Way, that teaches visiting students how to do all this as organically as possible. At the invitation of friends, I had visited a house church in Chesapeake, VA, and shared the vision of Blessings Hope. Many months later, when the opportunity came to Samuel to be trained in organic farming, this house church donated the tuition. Delighted, Samuel set out finding rides to the country of Zimbabwe. This was no simple matter. He was an exhausted, but excited young future farmer by the time he arrived! (It had been such an arduous and time-consuming trip, we wired him money so that he would be able to return home by plane.)

Samuel at Farming God's Way

Samuel found it to be invaluable training which he could not only share with his Blessings Hope farmers, but which he could pass on to other farmers in the region when he returned home. In fact, the principle of making decisions that would enhance the lives of the community and nation as well as Blessings Hope is deeply buried in Samuel's heart. He lives it out in every plan he makes. The dream is not *just* about today's orphans; it's about the future of his countrymen *and* his country.

It is amazing to watch how Samuel's passion to share the Gospel of Jesus Christ and the healing Jesus brings to broken lives affects the way in which he carries out his call. He is first and foremost an evangelist. It is his life blood. I sometimes don't hear from him for a week or two because he and his team are out in some remote village ministering to all who will listen—the curious, the sick and the spiritually hungry. Churches exist now where there had never been any. Miracles happen and believers are growing daily. Then he comes home and leads the Blessings Hope Healing Church which was birthed right there at Blessings Hope. Faith in Jesus Christ and his concern for the lost energize and drive every part of his life and leadership.

Reaching out to a remote tribe

Samuel baptizing a new believer

Samuel:

Today, as I walk around the grounds and see what God is doing at Blessings Hope Educational Centre, I see the fulfillment of his word in the book of Jeremiah 1:5, *Before I formed you in the womb of your mother I knew you*. So even before I had an idea, vision or dream, God had already planned this. So the key to developing an enduring and influential ministry is just to walk in God's plan and not turn back.

Chapter Five

It's Official!

For God did not give us a spirit of timidity, but a spirit of power, of love and of self-discipline. 2 Timothy 1:7

Samuel:

The year 2013 would prove to be historic. Blessings Hope Educational Centre would be dedicated and experience its first commencement! Our beloved Mum Joyce Strong, Sister Carol and Fay Martin (a friend of Mum's) were coming to officially dedicate Blessings Hope, speak to the children who were commencing and give them their certificates. Many people were going to celebrate the fulfillment of God's dream with us. The leaders from the local government also would join us and give their remarks on what God has done.

Joyce:

After having had only pictures from Samuel showing the building and growth of Blessings Hope, Carol, Fay (a long-time friend and supporter from Chesapeake, VA) and I couldn't wait to see the results with our own eyes! With tons of luggage filled with gifts and materials for the children, staff and teachers, and with the blessings of our spouses, we boarded the first of four connecting flights on our long journey to Kenya. We would be witnessing the children's first graduation celebration and taking part in the official Dedication of Blessings Hope Educational Centre.

Carol, Fay and I before takeoff for Kenya

Samuel and a delegation of students and teachers met us in the grassy field where our regional Kenyan 12-seater put down at the tiny Kitale Airport. Other folks who were awaiting arrivals were visiting in the shade of leafy trees on the perimeter or sitting patiently in the few chairs in the waiting room inside the airport.

As we stepped off the plane, the children began singing for us, welcoming us with smiles and then hugs and giggles.

So that you can better visualize where we actually were in Kenya, let me inject a bit of geographic and physical orientation into our story:

The Kitale Plateau is one of the most beautiful places in Kenya. It is situated in western Kenya, not far from the border of Uganda. Across arid land and directly northwest of Kitale is South Sudan; to the north is Ethiopia and farther east is Somalia and the Indian Ocean. Tanzania is the closest country to the south.

Resting in the Rift Valley between two mountain ranges and 5,988 feet above sea level, the Kitale Plateau is spared the severest droughts that many East African countries endure. The Plateau region boasts areas of rich farmland, lush greenery and trees filled with brilliant clusters of purple, orange or yellow flowers during much of the year, and experiences temperatures averaging 20 degrees F cooler than Nairobi. In some ways, it seems as though it lies in another world from the fast pace and modernity of Nairobi, the capital off to the southeast of Kenya.

Due to poverty and the lack of good jobs, people of the Kitale Region live very simply. In spite of hardship, I've never seen such wide and lovely smiles as in Kenya, especially in the rural area where Blessings Hope Educational Centre has blossomed.

Only about eight miles away from Blessings Hope is Kitale Town where there are restaurants, hotels, branches of Kenyan universities, banks and places to shop. Many supplies are needed to run the orphanage and school, so the relatively close proximity of the town is good. There are also medical clinics and a small government hospital in Kitale. For more serious medical needs, patients are taken to the larger city of Eldoret, which lies a few hours by car southeast of Blessings Hope.

It is a rare privilege for children to attend school in much of Kenya. Nothing is free: there are school fees, uniforms fees, and textbook fees regardless of whether it is a government school or a private school. Only orphanages offer a truly free education—usually only up through 8th grade—to orphans who live there. Most orphanages are supported by an established church conference. Some are supported by outside donors, especially in the first few years. Those who develop strategic farming projects and one or more small businesses on site become self-supporting. This is Samuel's goal.

The day of our arrival at Blessings Hope Educational Centre was sunny and warm, with a constant breeze that made everyone feel comfortable and carefree. Harvesting was in full swing and the rainy season was far behind now that November had arrived. The country was heading into summer when all is dry and the sun is at its equatorial hottest.

As Samuel's car crawled carefully through the narrow, pothole-pocked streets of the local village of Birunda on our way to Blessings Hope, folks stopped what they were doing and waved at us as we passed. Everyone knows Pastor Samuel. Even though we were running late, he stopped to chat briefly with anyone who approached the car.

Emerging from the other side of the town, we headed down a rutted dirt road framed on either side by lush vegetation and clearings within which nestled small mud or brick homes and a few tiny farms. Children popped out of their houses to watch us with great curiosity. Here and there, a lad would stand in characteristic fashion with one hand on his hip or staff and the other arm crossing his body at waist level, as he kept one eye on the nearby goats he was herding.

Finally, we reached the walled compound of Blessings Hope. The gates were already open, and neighbors and those passing on foot watched us with fascination. I got the feeling that they already knew that something amazing was about to happen inside those walls.

As our vehicle passed through the gates, children's voices burst into song! There they were— about 70 orphans in fresh, new tan and yellow uniforms topped with deep green sweaters bearing the Blessings Hope logo, and many teachers and staff members lining the driveway on both sides, singing their welcome to us. Even as they sang, the children watched our arrival intently.

Our welcome to Blessings Hope

Getting out of the car, we were immediately surrounded by a group of dancing women who drew us on to meet everyone. What a day of joy this was! As we moved slowly down the corridor of children, Carol, Fay and I fanned out to greet them one by one. Many were seeing white persons up close for perhaps the first time and weren't so sure about us! Their eyes were wide with wonder. The fearless broke into ready smiles.

As we reached the end of the welcoming lines and lifted our gaze to view the physical compound for the first time, we were amazed. The long classroom building, orphans' house, gazebo and cookhouse were truly grand. Painted and shiny, although still with dirt floors, each stood proudly side-by-side in a semicircle ahead of us. The outhouses were discreetly behind the buildings and nearly out of sight, but even they were brightly painted to match. In the open yard just inside the gates and to the right a huge, blue and white-striped tent had been erected to house the graduation and the conferences that would soon be upon us.

What a delight to gather in the largest classroom on the day of arrival and get to know everyone! First came the students and teachers who found a way to somehow all get into the room at once. I had a lot of fun sharing the story (a bit theatrically) of Paul and Silas in prison—how they sang and prayed in the worst of situations and God delivered them. The ground shook (which we acted out), the prison doors opened and they were free!

The best part of the story, though, was sharing the love of Jesus to the jailer and his family, who all became believers! I stressed to them gently that God doesn't waste *our* sorrows either, but redeems them and heals our broken hearts through his amazing love.

Students enjoying the story

Next, Carol, Fay and I met with the teachers and guardians and demonstrated how to give a verbal blessing to each other and to the children. Then I shared with Samuel a word from the Lord, a blessing that was intended specifically for him. (See *Samuel's Blessing* in Appendix B) It was a sweet, sweet time for all of us.

Finally, the volunteers and staff who do the farm and compound labor filed in. I had been longing for an opportunity to thank them for their hard work and faithfulness even in lean times, and to reminisce with them about some of the really hard jobs they had had to do. I had seen the pictures, but they had done the work. It was obvious that they were proud of what had been accomplished in just a few months, and rightly so!

Thanking the workers

We still had a little time before we needed to get back to our lodgings and prepare for the next day. So we took off in different directions, visiting and taking pictures of staff working, classrooms in session, kids laughing together in their dorm rooms and others piling onto the teeter-totter that a supporter had donated for the playground that was just inside the compound gate. (Have you ever seen 6-8 kids precariously balanced on each side of a teeter-totter, having the time of their lives? I can still hear their laughter!)

Then I darted out to see the animals that donors had provided: Grace and Mercy, the milk cows; the five goats that I had asked Samuel to lovingly name after members of my family, the baby chicks they were raising and the donkey and cart used to haul farm supplies. From there, I found the vegetable garden and the fields that had produced an admirable first crop of maize (corn) for eating and for seed for the next year. As I stood looking out over the fields, I was transfixed by the specter above them of the Mt. Elgon range in the distance, its rough ridges highlighted in the late afternoon sun. The beauty took my breath away.

Etched upon every single thing were the fingerprints of God. It took a long time to fall asleep that night.

Soil becomes modeling clay

Samuel with Grace and Mercy

Graduation Day dawned bright and clear. This time all the commencing children—in their graduation cloaks and mortarboards, with an added splash of color from the neck scarves we had given them the previous day—gathered up in town with the teachers and staff to form a procession. They would be led by the local Salvation Army Band playing "When the Saints Come Marching In" as they went on foot back down the long, one-lane, dusty road all the way to Blessings Hope. Carol, Fay and I cheated by riding in the lead car with Samuel. Neighbors, folks on bikes and motorbikes— with sometimes an entire family piled on—lined the road. Most smiled and waved at us as we passed, and some rode alongside us all the way. Some just stared.

Local children along the parade route

Ribbon-festooned and latched, black metal gates greeted us when we reached our destination. Pastor Samuel asked me to pray for Blessings Hope and cut the ribbon, declaring Blessings Hope Educational Centre officially dedicated and open for business! Then the gates swung wide, and the entire procession went through, ultimately assembling around a flag pole which stood in the yard between the orphans' house and the blue-and-white striped tent. After a brief welcome, a young student stepped forward in her graduation attire to solemnly raise the Kenyan flag and then lead us in saluting it, while the Salvation Army Band played the National Anthem.

After this, the children led us into the tent and then took their places in the front rows. Under the colorful canvas roof were local government guests; principals and head teachers from surrounding schools; pastors from churches near and far; staff, guardians and friends of the school—all excited to be part of this momentous occasion and check out this amazing place that had grown up out of the red clay field in only a single year.

For the children, it was the beginning of a long day of speeches, greetings, awards, singing and picture taking. Throughout each moment of it, the children were attentive and quiet and a bit in awe of it all. After a couple of hours, the teachers produced bottled drinks for them, which probably brought relief through all the speeches!

At last, Carol and I ceremoniously awarded the honor students with certificates while the Head Teacher described to the audience the outstanding work they had been doing and recited their final grades. With joy, I presented Samuel with a plaque that my husband had had engraved back in the U.S. to commemorate this very special day.

I've often wondered if the children slept that night. Were their heads so filled with memories of the sights and sounds that they just couldn't? Did they whisper to each other in their beds for hours? Did others slip quickly into dreams? The little ones—who had been totally bewildered by it all—probably fell asleep in relief as soon as their heads touched their mattresses. I *do* know that, as tired as I was, I hung onto consciousness as long as possible, savoring all I had seen and felt that day.

Saluting the Kenyan flag

Children with their certificates

At the end of a long day

Samuel with the plaque

Samuel:

During Graduation, my heart was overjoyed, and I was rolling with tears of joy to see the fulfillment of God's word for us. The children were so happy to be part of such a great privilege and honor.

This event has remained in their memories and inspires them to aim for great things in their lives. The entire Blessings Hope teaching and non-teaching staff were so encouraged to see the big miracle that God has done! Through all that, they came in one accord and declared that our God is "Ebenezer" (Heb. *Rock* or *Stone of Help*).

Joyce:

On Sunday morning after an early rain, the sky cleared and the sun shown brightly as people once again filled the tent. Immediately following a colorful and exuberant worship service that lasted several hours, it was time to dedicate the buildings. The entire congregation moved outside to witness Carol and Fay cutting the ribbons and officially opening the long classroom building and the orphans' house respectively.

I'll never forget the look on Carol's face later on when she sought me out in the crowd that was casually milling about after all the dedications were finished.

"I think God wants me to build a home for the widows!" she said with a light in her eyes. She had already called her husband Don back in Ohio, and he had agreed.

It made so much sense. I had always felt a bit odd whenever I read the key verse I used on all our brochures and much of my correspondence: "Religion that God our Father accepts as pure and faultless is this: To look after orphans *and widows* in their distress..." James 1:27. Caring for widows had been the missing part, and now God was speaking into Carol's heart to bring it to pass. How faithful is our God!

Samuel sent us pictures of the terrible living conditions of some of the widows whom he knew. He was overjoyed that Blessings Hope would be empowered to bring them out of poverty and abandonment and offer them a safe and meaningful future among the children and loving staff. He began immediately to make plans for the first widows' home.

The "home" from which Samuel would rescue one of the widows

Now I must share with you a special story about one of the youngest children.

Her name is Sharon. This little girl was about three years old at the time of that first graduation in 2013. She kept popping up in the different groups of staring or giggling children who followed me as I went from place to place around the compound. Yet whenever I tried to approach her, she ran for her life!

On Monday, just before I was to begin the afternoon sessions of the Women's Conference, who should come into the blue and white striped tent all by herself but Sharon! She marched straight up to me like a little soldier, looked me in the eye and then waited for me to respond. I tentatively reached out to her, hoping she'd not run away this time.

She didn't run. Instead she held her little hands out to me and let me lift her up into my arms as we sang. When I sat down, she was happy to sit on my lap and let me hold her near. She just kept looking into my eyes intently until suddenly, a little smile spread across her face. So we just smiled and smiled at each other until I had to speak to the women. When I set her down, she simply turned and marched out of the tent and back to her classroom.

I decided on the spot to sponsor her each month, and I couldn't wait to see her again. Since then, Samuel has always included her in the small group of students that he brings with him to meet our plane when we arrive. She is now six years old and in first grade, but she still is silent around me. But whenever I am walking on campus, she gets ahold of my hand and will not let it go until she absolutely must. When will she speak to me? When she is ready.

When I told the story to Samuel recently, he laughed and told me that her teacher had had a little talk with her about me earlier that day. I don't know what the teacher said, but it had completely relieved Sharon of her fear of me! I can't wait to see her again.

Just an aside: Carol and I both sponsor multiple orphans and teachers now. We decided right from the beginning that we would not show favoritism to "our orphans" when we visit or encourage other sponsors to send gifts to their orphans. Not all of them are sponsored yet, and many would be left out. We try however to take something small and special to *all* of the children each year. In 2013, we took brightly colored neck scarves that they donned immediately and didn't remove for days! I was amazed at how imaginative they were with those scarves.

More recently, Carol put together gift bags for all the children that contained glow sticks, suckers, note pads and pens. The children loved them.

Last year, I discovered an online Christian company that sells 3-5 inch-high stuffed wild animals common to Africa, plus sweet little white lambs that would be perfect for the youngest children. As small as the animals were, 100 of them nearly filled my largest suitcase. Somehow I still managed to squeeze in 100+ small toothbrushes and travel-size toothpaste tubes as well that had been collected and donated by a 4th grader from the Columbus area who loves to serve the needy wherever he finds them.

The children with their "wild animals" and lambs

While giving them their stuffed animals, I told them about how, as a child, I loved to hold such an animal in my arms as I fell asleep at night. I solemnly explained how their own little animals could play with them in their beds until lights out, and then they too could fall asleep with their new pets in their arms. Then in the morning, they must leave the little playmates by their pillows so that they would be right there when needed the next night. (This would ensure that the animals would stay clean and would not be lost outdoors. That would be a tragedy!)

For some crazy reason, I then instructed them how to respond if their animals "roared" at night. I lowered my voice, at which they all leaned forward to catch my counsel.

"Just say, 'shush!'" I whispered. "It's time to go to sleep!"

The next morning, I approached a group of children waiting for lunch to be served and asked them, "Where are your pets?"

"In our beds," they replied almost in unison.

"Very good!" I smiled. "Did any of them 'roar' in the night?" I asked very seriously.

"Oh, no!" they shook their heads definitively. "They were asleep!"

I caught myself before laughing aloud. By their expressions it was clear that this was no laughing matter! *Their* pets were very obedient!

Truthfully, tears well up in my eyes whenever I remember their joy at receiving those plush little pets. It was an amazing experience to witness their grave delight—if I might use those two words together—at receiving their first and very own stuffed animal. How I wished that *all* their sponsors could have been there too to enjoy that moment with us!

Chapter Six

The Dream Grows Amid Struggles

Jesus said: *"In this world you will have trouble. But take heart;*
I have overcome the world." John 16:33b

Joyce:

    A few months after our visit for that first Graduation and Dedication in 2013, the Minister of Health visited Blessings Hope and had some inconvenient news for Pastor Samuel. This time it was about the placement of a few of the buildings.

The official decided that the outhouse was too close to the cook house and had to be moved, and the cook house had to be rebuilt of brick. The gazebo couldn't be where it was either. I nearly cried when I heard that the gazebo had to be torn down! I gracelessly implored Samuel to find a way to reconstruct it wherever he could. Of course, he found a way! It is now located between the church and a small grove of trees where everyone loves to seek shelter from the sun or just relax and feel the wind filtering gently through the branches. Only a few yards on the other side of the grove is a lovely view of faraway, shadow-spotted Mt. Elgon.

The Minister of Works also appeared and wanted to be given the long-term plans for Blessings Hope and to see all the architectural drawings of any buildings that might go up later. Samuel was given just a few days in which to produce them. My first thought was, *How can he know in advance what God is going to say next?* But Samuel, always respectful and obedient, set to work with his engineer to plot out every possibility that might lie in the future. (Of course, this too took more money.) Judging by all the buildings that are now up and uncontested, Samuel obviously knew what he was doing!

By the summer of 2014, Carol and I were anticipating celebrating another graduation and ministering at Blessings Hope, and we began actively planning.

One sunny late-September day, when the foliage was brightening in fall transformation, I was out in my woods in Ohio asking God once again to show me what and how I was to minister at Blessings Hope in November. As I waited expectantly for an answer or impression from him, I had a dreadful experience! Everywhere I looked, the colorful woodland had inexplicably turned to grays and black. The leaves, trees, sun—all were shades of gray, and the ground was black and barren. The birds were silent and there was no breeze. It felt like death had taken over everything in sight.

That night I dreamed of exactly the same scene.

An ominous cloud descended upon us that prevented everything we had planned.

I told Carol that I had no peace about traveling to Kenya in November. God seemed to be warning us to stay home. So we cancelled our flights and tried to explain it to Samuel without scaring him. At the time, I had no idea why we were being warned.

It wasn't until sometime later that I learned from Samuel some of what was happening in Kenya during the time we would have been there. There was a heavy spiritual attack on his church in an attempt to divide it, curses spoken over his ministry and strange diseases among the animals. Samuel himself nearly died! Here is one of the emails that I received from him at the time:

Dear Mum,

I am so glad and feel the joy of God to hear from you. Surely I have been through a heavy battle with the devil which I didn't expect and which lasted throughout the week. Blood tests showed that there were more than seven types of diseases within me which were very strong and moving to attack my heart.

I think there was a time that I shared with you that I had not been feeling well. In fact, you had advised me to check with the doctor, but I bought only a pain killer. So after all this period I was attacked in a heavy way. Whoever saw me between Saturday and Sunday didn't believe I would live through it. My mum, wife and all the children together with the widows were crying. Some were reminding God of what I have been doing for the widows, orphans and the community. Through all these God heard their cries and healed me!

I was also surprised to hear that one of the orphans in our school, after seeing me in that critical condition, collapsed and even had to go to the hospital! He was discharged yesterday after rest.

You know, Mum, the devil had intended to go with one soul, but he didn't make it. All that he could do was kill one of our cows—the red one with a big body which you named Grace. Grace got sick on that Saturday morning, then by Sunday evening, she passed away. All this information I got today from my daddy. Everyone feared to tell me any sooner all that had happened for fear I might go into shock or have a heart attack. I was already shocked and my heart was in full pain as I was asking God many questions. Why had He allowed this to take place while He knew that the children really needed this cow for milk?

I have also been told that children had been crying throughout this time. Surely I miss them! While I was being told all these stories, I felt like flying and joining them, although I am still recovering slowly by slowly. Tomorrow I will go and meet them personally. Also pray for these children to be healed emotionally, since many, the way I heard the story, are really wondering, "Where is the love of God?" I know tomorrow I will have more time for counseling them, so pray with me for the wisdom and strength I will need, Mum.

From your son, Samuel

Whether Carol and I would have had an accident or been sick too, or simply been in the way during all the hardship, I don't know. The only thing that was clear was that we were right in heeding God's warning by staying home.

While we were rejoicing that Samuel was recovering, it was so hard to email supporters that dear Grace, the cow we had fallen in love with and dubbed our "Holy Cow" during fundraising for her purchase a year before, had died. Immediately, friends pledged money for her replacement. No one wanted the children to go without enough milk.

Samuel, always an astute shopper, found another that was pregnant (just as Grace had been last year). As in the case of Grace, he was purchasing two cows for the price of one. Mercy, the other cow that had been purchased last year, had been pregnant as well. In this way, a future herd was born.

We rescheduled our trip for January 2015, two months later. Even then, I didn't feel a lightness or delight in going as I usually did, but I felt that, short of another warning, we should go. Carol had many things she wanted to accomplish in getting to know the widows and gathering information from them. She also planned to get new pictures of the children for the Orphan Sponsors back home.

Meanwhile, I was scheduled to give a Women's Conference on Friday; speak briefly at Graduation on Saturday; preach on Sunday; interview teachers on Monday; and give a Couples' Conference on Wednesday through Friday. And so we went.

Everything was going well until Monday, the fourth day of our visit. Right after dinner, I got an email from my sister which bore shocking news. My dear elder brother Philip had died! His funeral would be on Friday in South Carolina. Could I come home? I didn't know how flights could be managed in such a short time, but I knew I had to go. That evening and all night, I was literally overcome by grief and denial. To this day, I cannot remember anything from the moment I received my sister's message until the next day when I could finally accept it.

Samuel heard the news and came over in mid-morning Tuesday as I was recovering. We discussed the ramifications of my leaving before the Couples' Conference that was to begin the next day and to which many people from several East African countries were coming. He was worried. There was no backup plan.

In the midst of my weakness, the Holy Spirit rose up and I clearly, firmly asserted that the Lord would minister even more powerfully in the next three days than we had hoped, if we would only trust him. He would raise up individuals from the audience who would have a word from the Lord for the people, and it would be the best conference they had ever had! I was sure of this! God's power had never depended upon *my* being there anyway.

There were no flights out of Kitale that day, so we would have to drive to the airport in Eldoret. In order to catch the plane out of Eldoret in time to leave that day for Nairobi and home, Carol and I had only one hour to pack and prepare ourselves for travel.

Pastor Isaac Gikonyo, who had been praying for me throughout the night before, contacted a pastor who would be able to take us to the airport. At the same time, Senator Zipporah Kittony, at whose farm we were staying, enlisted the help of her personal travel agent to chart a way home for us in a hurry. He took care of everything and by 3:00 that afternoon, we were loading our luggage into the pastor's car and heading to the airport in Eldoret.

I'll never forget that nail-biting ride! When we finally reached Eldoret, traffic slowed to a crawl. We zigzagged through the stalled rush hour traffic trying to find short cuts to the airport, which was on the other side of the city. With hearts pounding, we reached it just in time! That pastor was an amazing, faith-filled man who never doubted for a minute that we would make the flight.

From there, we caught the early evening flight to Nairobi and the 10:30 p.m. flight from Nairobi to Amsterdam. Then we flew to Detroit and on to Columbus and home. My husband Jim picked me up at the airport in Columbus around 9:30 Thursday night. By 11:00 p.m., I had showered and repacked a suitcase, and we were heading out the door for the 11-hour drive to my brother's church in South Carolina. The funeral would be at 11:00 a.m. the next day.

After losing some precious time on a wrong turn during the night, we arrived at the church just twenty minutes before the funeral was to begin! We quickly changed from traveling clothes into more appropriate attire and ran to the room where all immediate and extended family members were lining up to process into the auditorium to be seated. There was just time for a few hugs and tears before finding our place in the line.

The service was so healing! We experienced the most wonderful "Going Home" celebration of a much-loved, godly man who had ministered into hundreds of lives over the course of most of his life. It helped me walk through my grief and arrive at peace. How I had needed to be there!

Back in Kenya, the conference was a tremendous success. I had made the right decision to come home both for the sake of honoring my brother's wife and family, and for the sake of the Kenyans so that they could see God doing what only he can do.

By that summer, we sensed an "open heaven" to go and to expect good things, so we began making arrangements to travel in November. This time, Carol's husband Don would come too. He was anxious to see first-hand all he had been hearing about and what he had been helping support.

We had to land at the airport in Eldoret and be driven to Kitale, because flights were not available at that time to Kitale. This meant that the Blessings Hope entourage had to travel all the way from Kitale to Eldoret to pick us up! But Samuel never complained. Two vehicles came for us—the school van packed with a delegation of orphans and teachers, and a comfortable sedan driven by a good friend of Samuel's in which we were to ride. Everyone sang to us a sweet, sweet welcome song in front of the entrance to the airport. After lots of hugs, we were on our way.

Welcoming us at the Eldoret Airport

Pastor Samuel, knowing Don's keen interest in seeing the land that he had helped purchase for two future businesses that would soon help support Blessings Hope, took a slight detour to the site. It wasn't much to see yet, but the land was cleared and piles of bricks, stones and sand for making cement had been delivered. Looking at the simple scene through Samuel's eyes as he walked over the grounds and described his vision for the metalworking and tailoring businesses, we could imagine future craftsmen being trained, buildings full of commercial activity, and customers coming and going.

Samuel and his "Field of Dreams"

We couldn't stay long, so we quickly returned to the car and drove on to the main campus of Blessings Hope to greet everyone and prepare for the activities to come.

We were utterly amazed at how Blessings Hope had grown! It hit us full force as we stepped beyond the welcoming party inside the gates. The campus was actually becoming crowded with buildings! There were now an additional orphans' house, a second classroom building, Samuel's new home and a church! It is not surprising that the church building that Samuel's congregation had erected has had to be enlarged in less than a year due to the congregation's growth!

Blessings Hope Healing Church

Leadership Conference in the enlarged sanctuary

Second classroom building

Carol and Don with Blessings Hope widows

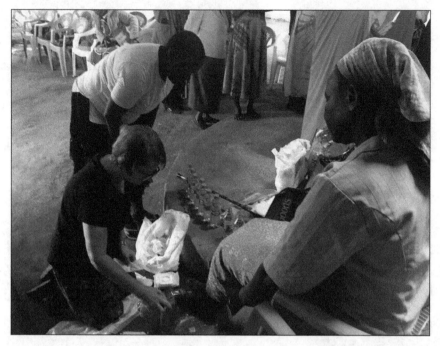

Carol washing widows' feet

Something we hadn't noticed when we arrived was a shop that had been built into the wall of the compound. Facing the street and to the left of the main gate, it will soon be a store from which the widows can sell produce, dry goods and small household items to people passing by.

When we returned in 2016, Carol met with not only Blessings Hope widows, but also widows from the Birunda village nearby. Many were interested in starting their own businesses. As widows, they need a sense of purpose and a means of supporting themselves.

Carol explained the financial and ethical principles that would be involved and asked them to draw up preliminary business plans. She reviewed them, selected the best plan and invested personally in it so that the widow could begin. This has inspired many widows to begin developing thoughtful, sensible plans that they can submit to

Carol whenever they are ready. Meanwhile, Carol has enlisted Pastor Isaac Gikonyo, a local pastor and friend of ours who has a passion to help the poor become self-sufficient, to offer them classes in business development as they move forward. Praise God!

Carol, BH widows and village widows in front of the widows' home

Friday, I spoke at the Women's Conference and Saturday, another joyous graduation celebration was upon us. This year, every child had successfully completed his or her class requirements and was advancing to the next grade level! Again, we had the honor of handing out certificates to the children as their progress was announced by the Head Teacher and cameras snapped away.

The Sunday morning sky was a delicate azure, without a cloud in sight. I loved the church service, rich with praise and worship—and lots of dancing. (I'm not quite sure what do with the video taken of me dancing with the worship team, but my extended family back in the U.S. sure got a kick out of it when they saw it after I returned home.)

My sermon was on preparing for inevitable persecution by pursuing God with all our hearts. Jesus promised his disciples, and thus us, that the Holy Spirit will give us the words to say when the time comes. Our task is to live at rest in the shadow of the cross, knowing the power of God's love and forgiveness for us and the world. Our strength will come by spending time in his Word and listening for his voice before serving others. It's in his presence that we find freedom from fear!

Preaching that morning

After church, everyone moved outside. Carol and Don cut ribbons on the widows' house—already full of grateful women who now have a loving family and fresh purpose—and the new classroom building. They shared their hearts at each location as everyone gathered around. The atmosphere was charged with wonder.

As often happens in mid-afternoon in Kenya, the skies began to change. Massive dark clouds were moving in from the southwest, so we quickly went on to Samuel and Sharon's new home, which I officially dedicated and blessed. (See *House Blessing* in Appendix B) After the blessing, everyone poured through the house, examining every room and exclaiming how wonderful it was. As I moved with the crowd from room to room, I could imagine Samuel and Sharon's children—as well as visitors and even pastors on retreat—filling each room with life and laughter.

Samuel's new home

When we returned to the living room, friends and visitors were relaxing on the couches that lined all but one wall of the spacious room. Everywhere, inside and outside the house, folks were chatting warmly and laughing often. What I loved best about Samuel's home was the magnificent view of the fields and mountains from the back patio. What a lovely place to dream, reflect and pray!

Meanwhile, mounds of dark clouds were lumbering in, portending a strong afternoon rainstorm. But only the three of us Americans seemed concerned as everyone else leisurely strolled back to the church for some final words from Bishop Michael Wafula. I must admit, however, that Carol and I especially breathed a sigh of relief when the downpour held off until after the meeting and we had safely entered the car that would take us back to the hotel. Then the skies seemed to erupt with glee.

Samuel:

Thinking of the church and my new home leads me to thank God for my parents, Bishop Michael and Rev. Phipian Wafula, for the good foundation they laid in my life. I can remember and list the four principles which they gave me at the age of twelve:

1. Love God more than anything
2. Be faithful in every area of my life
3. Be a person of integrity
4. Care more for other's needs than for my own.

Sincerely speaking, these principles have been the pillars of my life. By observing them, God's blessings have been overflowing on my way.

I can remember very well as I started the ministry that I had nothing, and my aim was just to move across the globe and share the love of God. In my poverty, I remained faithful in serving God, and my love for him continued to grow and become stronger every day. Even though I faced difficult situations because of spreading God's word, my focus, vision and dreams never changed. In every situation, the fire within me continued to burn.

Because of my parents' fourth principle, whenever I got anything, first I made sure to share with the orphans and those in need. Due to my faithfulness, God opened doors and gave me responsibility for money. Still, the flow of money didn't change the power of my dad's principles in my life. You can imagine: while I was being sent money from Mum Joyce to buy the land for the school, build the classrooms, erect widows' and orphans' houses and meet the children's needs, my own family was staying in a rental house. We could be locked out by our landlord at any time. However, my focus was just to accomplish what the money had been sent for. As I was doing all this, I didn't know that great fruit would come from it for my life and family.

While living in rental houses, we faced a lot of challenges. Sometimes while I was gone on a mission to the villages, I would get a call from my wife telling me that the landlord was closing us out of the house because we were late with the rent. This issue really disturbed my heart. I came to discover that the devil was using that chance to discourage me while in the ministry. But this challenge also brought me into the presence of God. I spent much time in prayer asking God to make a way so that my family could have a place to settle in safety in our own home. Whenever I was praying and declaring this, I felt the peace of God and knew that God was working out something for his glory.

Staying in a two-bedroom rental house due to my poor income had really limited me in hosting visitors. In addition to my family, we were also taking care of more than ten children, so whenever the visitors came, they could only sleep in the sitting room. Sometimes I asked help with space from my neighbor, which was not convenient for his family. But all the time I knew that one fine day God would make a way out for his glory.

At one point, my daddy gave me a very small room which he had built for my younger brothers at his ministry in Kiminini. So we moved there. However, I was not comfortable with that arrangement. It was a big challenge for me to be traveling every day to work at Blessings Hope then traveling home again in the evening. So due to this I could only come home to see my family once a week or whenever I could get a ride. My heart wanted for me to be with my family, so I kept on praying and trusting upon God. I was reminded by the Holy Spirit that God always makes a way where there seems to be no way.

Then one fine day, God spoke to Mum Joyce about building us a house. She asked me to draw up plans that would not only meet our needs but would have plenty of room to offer rest to pastors and friends who might come. It was like a dream! Our hearts were full of joy and our mouths were filled with laughter to see what God was about to do.

The night before the day on which we were supposed to break ground for the house, I was lying in bed and sensing Someone speaking to me. I was being reminded of my parents' four principles. Then a soft voice whispered into my heart about our place of worship. I realized that God wanted me to do something since our place of worship (a classroom) was very small and our people needed to build a church. I didn't discuss it with anybody, but when morning came, I told our engineer to set up the church first. My house could follow later.

That's what took place, and my heart was filled with great joy. So we started church construction. After we were done with the roof, we went back to build my house. I bless the name of our living God for supplying the materials and funds for the completion. Right now we have five bedrooms in a single family house on the grounds of Blessings Hope, with a spacious sitting room, kitchen, garage, prayer room and office. Surely God is amazing and his timing is the best.

During the official opening of the church and my house, surely I saw God. My heart was thumping with a lot of joy. In fact, I don't know how I can express how it happened, but above all, I know that God is always faithful and ready to accomplish what he starts. (See *Church Blessing* in Appendix B)

When I see my house and all that has been established here, I see the glory of God. Also my heart has never stopped praying for those people who are still in rental houses as I was, for surely they face a lot of hardship. As I believe God remembered me, he will also remember them in their situations.

My great appreciation goes to God for providing all the finances and to our dear Mum Joyce and Daddy Jim for hearing God's voice and making all this come through. Thanks to our partners, Sister Carol, her husband Brother Don and all Joyce Strong Ministries supporters. We love you and we are proud of what God has led you to do. May God's grace be upon you all in the name of Jesus of Nazareth, amen.

Joyce:

After all the celebrations and dedications, the day came for the Leadership Conference at Samuel's father's ministry in Kiminini, the same place at which I had spoken in 2012—the year I had met the children in the field. While I was teaching, Carol and Don were back at Blessings Hope spending time with the widows (including ones who came to meet them from town), securing updates on the children who already had sponsors, and photographing as many unsponsored children as time permitted.

On Tuesday, our last day there, I would finally have time with the teachers, staff and students. Praise God! As we traveled by car to Blessings Hope that morning, I worshipped quietly, ignoring the gentle banter of the others in the car. My heart was so hungry for a space apart in God's presence! The music that our driver and friend Roy was playing on the car's CD player was from the 70's when the Holy Spirit was being poured out in the U.S. I knew every song, and the Holy Spirit was ministering to me through each one.

When we arrived, I tried to get out of the car with everyone else, but couldn't. The tears came and I couldn't stop crying for a very long time. Samuel stayed with me but had the wisdom to say nothing, as all the intensity of ministering during the past four days was being released and burdens lifted. I had absorbed the cries of so many hearts, and seen so much sorrow and joy jumbled together, that I was just too full to go on until it was all emptied into the lap of Jesus. Samuel understood and patiently waited. I would dry my eyes and try to exit the car many times only to fall back into the car sobbing.

Finally, the transfer was complete. My heart was again free to be be present and open to receive whatever would happen that day. Life was simple again. Hope and joy quietly reigned.

During the past 20 years of international ministry especially, I've found that this process is necessary. Even after the most fruitful, exciting trips, I am useless and given to despondency until I can go to the woods alone to weep and cry out to God. Always he takes the weariness and my myriad experiences upon himself. He refreshes my heart and enables me to return to the human race.

Every person in ministry must learn the power of solitude with God and the need to be emptied and refreshed in his presence. If we don't learn it, we will either grow numb or live on a roller coaster emotionally. Ultimately we will grow sick of people and their problems, depressed and want to give up.

Small offenses will become as mountains, and our own weaknesses will be exploited by Satan. Soon *we* will be the offenders! We must learn that we cannot bear being part of so many lives without finding relief. We were not created to do so. We were created to rest in him.

After coming to rest that morning at Blessings Hope, I was able to leave the car, smiling. I couldn't wait to meet with the teachers and staff and play with the children! My only fear was that this precious time would pass all too quickly. But it was as though time stood still! The two scant hours I had free to be with them mysteriously stretched into what seemed like many of pure joy!

On this visit, we were brought face to face with the fact that the children were growing up fast! Last year, there were just a few in high school, and only two entering college. Since Blessings Hope school goes only through elementary school, funds had to be raised each year for all the tuition and fees required by the area high schools. When there were just a few students at that level, fundraising hadn't been difficult. But that January, there would be *thirteen* in high school, and *three* in college. After that, the rate would really accelerate as more and more moved up.

In 2013, we had founded an Orphan Sponsorship Program, and half of the children now have sponsors. *Our prayer is that by 2018, all eighty orphans will be sponsored.* When we returned home, I promptly set up a Scholarship Fund as well for high school and college students in anticipation of what we will face in the years ahead. That fund is now in operation, and the donations that are received are of tremendous help to the children in their pursuit of a new and greater future.

High school students in 2016

Part Two

THE CHILDREN'S DREAMS

Chapter Seven

Love, Safety and Care

Let them give thanks to the LORD for his unfailing love and his wonderful deeds for men, for he satisfies the thirsty and fills the hungry with good things. Ps. 107:8-9

Samuel:

*B*lessings Hope Educational Centre is an admirable place for everyone. It's a place full of love, safety and care. When children are new here, I always take a moment to speak with them and to know their hearts about learning and staying at Blessings Hope. Not one has ever given me a negative word. They are proud to be part of this great family where their spiritual and physical needs are met.

What we are providing at BH is more than what most parents can provide for their children at home especially at this hard time when our economy is very poor. We provide them with all meals and special diets; clothing and shoes; and an excellent education and health care. Many tell me that they love Blessings Hope because of the Christian foundation we have built as well as the true love and care we are showing them.

I appreciate my entire team and staff for serving with me faithfully and revealing the love of Jesus Christ of Nazareth to these children. Because of all this and the freedom they have been given to practice their gifts and talents, these children feel that Blessings Hope is the best and warmest home for them. It's our daily prayer that God will continue to expand this centre as we seek to touch many generations for God's glory.

To understand the dreams of the children, we must first have some comprehension of what many of them endured before being rescued.

Faith's story:

"I have two older siblings and two younger ones. When I was only six years old, my mother died and my father disappeared. I remember the darkness of those days and the fear in which we lived as we were split up among relatives. In some of these homes, we were not safe. In others, relatives wished we would all just die and leave them alone. The chief of our village denied us our mother's property and refused to even admit we were from his village. We had no one to defend us.

"As soon as I could, I rescued my younger siblings from the dangerous homes they were in and took them to my grandmother's on my mother's side. There we were safe, but destitute. Then one wonderful day, Bishop Michael Wafula, Samuel's father, heard about us and took us into his home. Even though he was very poor himself, and his children (including Samuel) had little to eat, he and his family shared with us whatever they had and kept us safe. Best of all, they shared with us the love of Jesus.

"In 2012, Pastor Samuel opened Blessings Hope Educational Centre, and all five of us were brought here. At Blessings Hope, my siblings and I are thriving! We have been given hope and a future.

We now know who we are! We are children of God, precious and created for a wonderful reason.

"My older siblings, Edwin and Nelly, completed high school and are in college studying to be doctors, all because of the generosity of supporters of Joyce Strong Ministries and the excellence and love of Blessings Hope. I graduated this year from high school and will begin college in January of 2017. I too want to enter the field of medicine, but I want to become a surgeon and someday build a hospital that will have all the best equipment and help those like me who have suffered so much in the past."

Faith

Joyce:

I have never gone to bed hungry—not even once in my life. When Pastor Samuel shared stories with me of his own childhood in which they did well to have one meal a day of rice or vegetable and ugali, I began to think in an entirely different way about the role of food in the life of a believer.

I was amazed that he never complained about such deprivation. As I have watched him through hard times, I have realized that doing without has created a dichotomy of freedom and compassion in his life. *For one thing, he is free to care more about others than himself.* For instance, when we visit Blessings Hope and mealtime comes around, he is busy making sure everyone else is cared for, and he has to be reminded that he must himself sit down and eat. His own hunger doesn't control him.

His freedom is also obvious whenever there is a crisis at Blessings Hope. The first thing he and the leaders do is fast and pray, often late into the night and sometimes for days. They don't give it a thought. They know where the power really comes from and they just do it. They are free. Samuel personally counts it a privilege to spend time in intense fellowship with God. Food is forgotten.

The other side of the dichotomy is evident in his passion to see that hungry children are not only fed regularly, but fed nutritiously. Whenever I visit the children, there is not a single one who is skinny or ravenous at mealtimes. They are healthy, energetic and bright-eyed. When mealtime comes, they wait patiently in line for their turn to receive their food and then just enjoy it and each other as they eat.

Incidentally, for the first year and part of the second, until their farm produced enough food, my ministry partners helped Blessings Hope purchase rice and corn in bulk at the market. In 2016, however, the Blessings Hope farm provided enough food to feed the children, staff and visitors, with extra left over to sell at the market and buy seed for the next year! They only needed our help to buy fertilizer.

We thank God for the healthful food and balanced diet the children at Blessings Hope receive. Here is a sample of their menu for a typical week:

Monday through Wednesday:
Upon rising at 6:30 a.m.—a cup of tea and mandazi.
Breakfast at 10 a.m.—porridge
Lunchtime at 12:45 p.m.—mix of beans and maize
4 p.m.—evening tea
Supper at 7:30 p.m.—ugali and cabbage or sukuma

Thursday through Saturday:
Upon rising at 6:30 a.m.—a cup of tea and an egg
10 a.m.—porridge
Lunchtime at 12:45 lunch—rice and beans
4 p.m.—evening porridge
Supper at 7:45 p.m.—ugali, meat or fish, sukuma or cabbage

Sunday:
Breakfast at 6:30 a.m.—a cup of tea, an egg, a piece of mango or orange
12:45 pm lunch—mixture of beans and maize
4 p.m.—a cup of tea or porridge
Supper at 7:45 p.m.—beans, chapatti and rice

This is a carefully planned and nutritious menu that is not possible for many Kenyans. Blessings Hope is so grateful for the farmland, milk cows, goats and chickens that donors have provided to help make good nutrition possible! The staff at Blessings Hope are excellent stewards of these assets and produce or grow most of their food right there.

I've often wondered how Samuel and the staff could so effectively absorb children of all different kinds of experiences of loss and different ages into "one family." How did they learn to bring such healing and peace into the children's lives? He answered my question thoughtfully.

Samuel:

Dealing with kids is very hard, especially during the times they might be facing challenges. This is why I ask our teachers and all supporting staff members to join me before we start our day in asking God to give us the Spirit of wisdom, revelation, understanding and counsel. Without these, there is no way we can sufficiently answer all the questions which we may encounter as we take care of these kids.

If there are people who can ask you anything when you least expect it, it is these kids, and most of the time, they need an instant answer. And so I would like to share with you a couple of stories of when I have been questioned by kids while they were facing challenges or when they have been lonely, homesick or afraid.

About two years ago, we lost one of our milking cows, many chickens, a sheep and a goat. It was a hard moment for me to answer questions. I can really remember well when a Class One child who was about six years old came to me and asked me a very hard question.

"Pastor Sam, my heart is full of pain. Within the shortest moment, we have lost our milking cow, chickens, goat and sheep. Do you think that God always hears our prayers?"

After a pause, he continued, "Most of the time before we go to bed or after we wake up in the morning, you tell us to pray for our teachers, supporters, our friends our animals and even our nation that God may give us peace and unity. So why has all this happened? Doesn't God know that we need the eggs and milk? Since the death of our cow and chickens, we have not been getting enough milk and eggs. Please, I would like to know your answer."

After he had asked me this, he stood patiently waiting for my response. I told him, "God knows everything and he knows that we need milk and eggs. But sometimes he may allow Satan to test our faith to see if we will still trust him when we miss taking a cup of tea or eating an egg. Shall we still love and serve him?

"Sometimes God can take us out of our comfort zone to see the percentage of our love for him. Many people pray and declare their love for God when they have everything, but once they might miss or lack something, then they reduce their love for God. It's been this way from the beginning of time."

Then I shared with him the story of Job in the Bible and about what happened to him and the reward he got after remaining faithful. The boy was very happy for the response. I also encouraged him to keep loving God and remaining faithful in his daily prayers as we look forward to God's provision and replacement.

Through this child's question, my eyes were opened, and I took a moment to encourage all of the children. I sensed in my spirit that there were many who might have the same questions.

Concerning sickness and loneliness, 2015 was a very hard year. We had never experienced so much sickness as then. In many areas of the country, there were breakouts of malaria, which prompted new questions.

One morning around 9:30 a.m., I was sitting in our woods, which is just within our school compound and near my home site. Linda, who is 11 years old, came to me and asked permission to ask me a question. I told her that she could.

She began, "Daddy, it has been very hard for us to enjoy our studies because most of our friends are sick. If we go to our dormitories right now, more than ten people are on their beds. Do you think that we have sinned against God and that's why He has allowed all this sickness to happen to us?"

Here I realized that I could not be neutral. If I said, "No," then she might take me back in the Bible to where God allowed plague, sickness and suffering when the children of Israel or other people sinned against him. So I told her that sometimes such can happen.

"But we must also consider what the change of weather does to us," I continued, "as well as our ignorance, which can cause sickness. Most of the time during the rainy season, we have many mosquitoes. Sometimes we walk outside during the evenings when they are biting, and sometimes we play in water where they live. Sometimes we ignore sleeping under our mosquito nets. So due to all these, we get sick."

So I advised her to be careful to follow all the instructions that the matron has been giving them to avoid becoming sick. I also told her that the rest of the children will be okay since they are under medication and because we pray for them. She was very happy and left with a big smile on her face.

Lastly, as I think back to the beginning of our school and home, I remember that we had many children who were dramatically affected by their pasts. Many of these children witnessed their parents being killed and their sisters and mothers being raped. This really caused them to hate people and to lose hope and peace.

I just want to thank God for giving me a great staff, for it has been very difficult for us to answer a lot of the questions which these children have been having. We have learned to pray together daily for wisdom, and I am so blessed to write that since the beginning of Blessings Hope until now, we have seen a very great change. God has truly imparted life and hope into the lives of these children.

In the beginning, it was not uncommon to find an orphan child sitting outside behind the classrooms, maybe shedding tears or sitting in silence. What really challenged us was that most of the children could not open up their hearts and share with us. So in whatever situation we might find them and ask what was wrong, they might tell us, "Nothing. I am just relaxing." If we asked why they were not playing with others, they might tell us, "I am tired." If we asked why they were crying, they might pretend that something had fallen into their eyes. So it was very difficult to know what such children were undergoing.

I realized that we needed high wisdom and the Spirit of God to help us so that we could help them. So I called upon all of my staff. I talked with them, and we prayed together and declared the book of Isaiah 11:1-3 to be part of our lifestyle. God gave us the revelation to start making friends with these children, bringing them gifts and showing them great love, care and concern. By doing all these, they started to open up their hearts and share their stories. We learned about their challenges and what was making them withdraw. When

89

we discovered such things, it was a high moment. We spent much time with them, became close friends, played together and shared stories and God's word. Just within one day, it was normal for us to interact with them like this perhaps three times.

Through all these means and the effective prayers of the believers and staff, we have seen God bring great changes in their lives. We also realized that each teacher needs to be like a parent in his or her classes. Through all these means, we have seen great fruits. So we bless God because it's by his wisdom that we are able to meet the desires of their hearts and bring back the love, joy and hope which they had lost.

Joyce:

Samuel's wife Sharon factors greatly in the climate and heart of Blessings Hope. She is a gentle, smiling, young woman who offers no pretense at all. She draws no attention to herself, yet is a joyful delight to be with. God gave me a glimpse into her heart and character back in 2015 before we ever actually had a conversation. I wrote down what I saw and then surprised her at the Women's Conference that year by calling her up and speaking it to her as a blessing. (See *Sharon's Blessing* in Appendix B) She wept off and on for several hours afterward. I then saw the validity of what God had shown me. There is a depth to her love and character that is unusual and perfect for the calling on her life.

I had gleaned from Samuel's emails that the children are often in their home to visit and can freely approach him or his wife with any question or problem they are having. So I asked Sharon if she ever gets tired of having children in and out of her house and if she would rather have more privacy.

The question startled her, and she quickly replied, "No, Mum, no! I never get tired of them! I love them as though they are my own children. I am happy to be with them at any time and would not want to live apart from them." By the way that her face glowed when she spoke of them, I felt silly and small-hearted for having even asked the question. So I changed the subject and we talked of other things.

However, this week I wrote to Samuel and asked him to have her write a response to a question that wouldn't seem so peculiar to her: "What is it like being a mother to all these children?"

I received her response the very next day:

Dear Mum Joyce,

What a glorious blessing to be mum to so many children! It always touches my heart as I stand alongside my husband to support and mentor these precious kids. It's very hard work if you don't have God's calling and a heart of love and care. But we do.

If there is something I especially like in my life, it's always being with these kids. They have become a gift to me, and I am in love with them. This is why most of the times when my husband Pastor Sam may wish me to go with him for maybe a week-long mission, the first words and thoughts which always come to my mind are how much I would miss these kids, their jokes, smiles and stories. So due to that, I always excuse myself so that I can stay with them.

Spending time with these kids from the beginning has caused my relationship with God to be very strong. Always whenever we share stories and jokes and play together, I laugh and even cry as I remember how far God has brought them. He has delivered them from shame, danger and the painful life they had been undergoing.

All of this brings me close to God and causes me to keep praying for them that God may accomplish their visions and dreams.

Above all, I am so blessed and thank God for our Joyce Strong Ministries partners who stand alongside us to see that we accomplish what God has called us to pursue. Through your support and prayers, God is doing amazing things. May God's peace be with you."

Sharon with daughter Ellen

Chapter Eight

A Fine Education and a Good Future

In all your ways acknowledge him, and he will make
your paths straight. Proverbs 3:6

Joyce:

    *J*n 2014, Edwin and Nelly, brother and sister to Faith, graduated from high school. Both were excellent students, testing well in college entrance exams and electing to study medicine with the goal of becoming doctors. Supporters of my ministry gave wholeheartedly and supplied the needed funds for their educations.

When Edwin heard that he would be able to attend college debt free and fulfill his dream of becoming a doctor, he was overcome. He shared the good news and his gratitude with the student body and staff during chapel and wept for joy. He promised the Lord before all in attendance that he would donate 40% of his income as a doctor to Blessings Hope to help other children succeed as he had. That was an amazing promise for this young man to make. It revealed the depth of his love for Blessings Hope and his gratitude for all he had received. How it inspired everyone! Soon all the children were crying with him and committing to do the same no matter what their profession would be in the future.

Edwin and Nelly

Edwin Marshall, in his own words:

I humbly thank God for how far he has brought me. What I have received at Blessings Hope spiritually, educationally and socially is really amazing, and I wonder how I can explain it.

I have been taught so much about our supreme God who is to be worshiped and praised, and I have been challenged to live a morally upright life. My faith has been made bold through the teachings that I have received which have helped me to understand the Word of God better, and I have given myself to Jesus as my personal Savior. I am a staunch believer, and I am addicted to the Word of God from which I have been able to discover my gifts and talents. By the grace of God, I can compose songs, sing, lead prayer and play some instruments in the church.

Blessings Hope has been a great blessing to my life. The evangelism that we have been doing during my free time during semester breaks from college has really inspired my life. I have not only been practicing my ministry, I have made new friends, which has helped me to continue growing socially. The outreach mission that we have been doing has increased my courage to speak fluently in the congregation without trembling. So I thank God for all that he is doing on my way through Blessings Hope. It's my prayer that God will bless all who have stood alongside Blessings Hope to make a difference in my life.

Before I entered Blessings Hope, I was miserable! But now I have hope and my life has a bright future. All my basic needs have been met, which is like a dream to me. I have been educated from a high school level to a college level, which I didn't expect would happen. Blessings Hope has provided everything for my good. I thank God for showing great concern and love for my life. I believe that my vision and mission will come through and that I will make a big difference in someone else's life too. Thanks to all and Shalom.

Joyce Strong:

I have asked a few high school students to share their stories as well, especially about how they have grown spiritually and socially, and how Blessings Hope has been good for them.

Ruth Chepwemoi:

What a great privilege for me to be part of the Blessings Hope family! Wow, it was truly a great honor to be selected from among the needy millions of children across our country to attend here! I thank God for it and I can't take it for granted.

Blessings Hope is a great place to be, and I can't even count all the great things that it has done for me. I have been grown both spiritually, academically and socially. The knowledge that I receive about Jesus Christ while I attend lunch hour prayer meetings and church services has greatly strengthened me, and I have accepted Jesus Christ as my personal Savior. I have also met different children and adults from different tribes with different characteristics, which has helped me grow socially and learn to love without prejudice.

Thanks to all who are sacrificing and supporting me. In fact I never dreamed that one of these fine days I could step into high school! What God is doing is amazing. Right now I am in high school, where I am committed to studying very hard to see that I achieve my dreams.

May God bless you all for providing me shelter, food, love and security. Blessings Hope is the perfect place for me to be. May God bless all staff and our Director Pastor Samuel.

Selly Chepkosikei:

Hi, I am in my third year of high school. I truly wonder where I can start to express my great joy and warm feelings towards Blessings Hope, for what this place has done in my life is really wonderful. I have acquired spiritual knowledge, and through the evening prayers and morning devotions that we normally have daily, God has taken my life from one level to another. The church services that I attend every Sunday in Blessings Hope Healing Church have greatly impacted my life. I have learned how to pray and even lead the church service. Above all, I have learned how to open the Scripture in the Bible and share it with my fellow children.

Blessings Hope has given me opportunity to study with different people from different communities in our country, hence enlarging my social life and helping me understand others. Blessings Hope has cared for my education by paying my high school fees and other things required by the school. I continue with my studies comfortably.

Blessings Hope provides for all my needs. My life has been changed through the great support that I receive, and I always pray that God may continue the great unity that is in our midst. I look forward to accomplish God's plans for my life.

I am very blessed to be at Blessings Hope since it is laying a good foundation in my life. God bless Mama Joyce for standing alongside Pastor Sam to bring change in our lives and healing to our wounded souls. We love you!

Samuel:

As you know, Blessings Hope is made up of children from different regions, cultures and religions. Most of them are orphans or destitute, abandoned street children. So these children did not come from comfort. Many were wounded by their parents, friends, guardians and neighbors, and each of the children brought a different story. It has been our task to overcome their early painful memories and instill new life in their hearts.

Through the help of the Holy Spirit and the cooperation of our staff, we have united these children and they have become one family. The major strategy that my team uses is all about becoming friends to them, listening and sympathizing with their situations; protecting their rights; and showing them true love and care. Through all these we have seen positive responses in their lives. Praise God!

Always it touches my heart to see that I am connected to and working with God-fearing people. The Blessings Hope teaching and non-teaching staff are doing a great job. They are not only serving and teaching the children, but also healing their hearts by helping them through the pain of great losses or abuse from the past.

Our Head Teacher Peter gave me an example recently of how this works: "When a child withdraws, it is usually through sadness, anger or homesickness. You can help him or her by gently finding out what the problem is and then trying to solve it through counseling.

"For instance, a child of a single parent came to school one day but looked emotionally disturbed. I was kind and friendly to her and asked her why she was not feeling well and not in her usual mood to study. Because of the relationship we have built, she felt safe and free to tell me that she had been beaten brutally by her mother in the past. I continued to be gentle with her and was able to comfort and counsel her. After that, she began to relax and enter into the class."

Joyce:

The stories are as numerous as the children. At Blessings Hope, healing comes—sometimes slowly, sometimes quickly. As it does, they begin dreaming for themselves for the future because hope has been born in their hearts. Here are some of their dreams:

- Derrick Wafula wants to be a pastor as well as a doctor. He loves God and likes praying and telling people about the Word of God, and he also wishes to provide good care and treatment to God's people.

- Anita Wangila would like to be a lawyer because she wants to defend innocent people and promote justice.
- Linda Mukhwana would like to be a teacher because teaching is her passion and she would like to be a blessing to others.
- Another child says that she would like to be a doctor because she wants to treat deadly diseases and restore the health of people and lengthen people's life spans.
- Cynthia Wanjala said she would like to be a nurse because she wants to serve patients with kindness and ensure they get treatment in a healthy, friendly and clean environment.
- Vance Dawayi said he would like to be a mechanic because he wants to maintain people's vehicles in good condition, and to ensure continuous economic development by helping the owners to be at their work places on time.
- Geoffrey Sakwa would like to be a teacher because he wants to pass knowledge to people with the purpose of improving lives and fighting illiteracy that breeds ignorance.
- Griffin Wangila says he wants to be a magistrate because he wants to decide cases and to promote justice.
- Samuel Okwale would like to be a bishop because he wants to take care of the flocks of God. He wants to help people know the Word of God and serve him.
- Mildred Adour would like to be a neural surgeon because she wants to separate twins who are joined physically at birth.

These are a very consistent sample of the hopes and dreams of the children at Blessings Hope Educational Centre. God is raising up a "new generation" of dreamers who have his heart for the world and his love in their hearts, and he has made this possible through this amazing place of miracles.

Joyce:

During 2016, there was a breakout of school fires all over Kenya which were lit by the very students who attended. I was shocked and puzzled when I read about them in newspapers here in the U.S.

In November when I was in Kitale, I asked Peter, the Head Teacher, to find out for me what the Blessings Hope high school students who study off campus think about the crisis. He was to ask them what they felt were the reasons the students would burn their own schools, why their particular high school was spared, and how peace could come to the schools that were burned.

Peter reported that the causes were perceived to be:

1. Poor food
2. Harsh treatment by teachers
3. Poor attitude of teachers toward students
4. Abrupt raising of school fees
5. Poor performance by students and the schools

Blessings Hope students believed that their own school was spared because:

1. It has good leadership
2. The teachers are friendly to them and care about them
3. The school is performing well
4. Students are given the freedom to choose their own class leaders

When asked how peace could be established in Kenyan schools, the students replied:

1. By teachers creating good relationships with the students
2. By providing an environment conducive for learning
3. By listening to the views raised by the students

It's interesting that their observations reflect the values that they had absorbed while in grade school at Blessings Hope Educational Centre.

The Social Workers who have been serving at Blessings Hope would like to share their observations of the strengths of the school and staff and their personal experience of being there.

Esther Kusiero, Social Worker:

My view of the teaching methods at Blessings Hope is really positive. We have qualified teachers who are giving their time generously to the children. They offer extra time to come and help the kids even during evening prep time. The teachers who come from outside are really trying to support the children. Some teachers bring in their own ideas which are being implemented, and these facilitate big changes. The performance of our children is very good compared to our neighboring schools. In 2015, we were rated #2 in the region. This year, we hope to be #1. The entire staff and students have worked very hard to achieve such a rating.

Regarding spiritual growth, I personally have made big steps compared to where I was some years back. Being here has changed my life! I have been instructed and blessed by the lunch hour prayers which we normally have on Thursdays as a whole staff. The teachings are really encouraging and up-lifting. Also the pupils' sessions which we hold on Fridays have made me grow spiritually.

Regarding leadership, the school exercises a good plan whereby we have heads of departments, under which different offices are assigned to tackle different issues. In general, the environment is good and admirable.

Eunice Nakhumicha, Social Worker:

It is my great pleasure and joy to give you my observations of the strength of Blessings Hope Educational Centre.

Blessings Hope Educational Centre is founded in God's heart, and it relies on him. There is nothing which has ever taken place or been done to solve any differences without consulting God. Due to this, it has been revealing the great ministry of God and his joy in our midst.

Also I am seeing God accomplish the words of King David in the book of Psalms 28:7 "The LORD is my strength and my shield; My heart trusts in him, and I am helped; therefore my heart exults, and with my song I shall thank him."

Blessings Hope is a special and unique centre compared with other schools. It's a place where children are taught good behavior and respect and are molded, trained and empowered to be an effective and God-fearing generation. It really also touches my heart that when I enter the Blessings Hope compound, I can feel the love and presence of God. It's a centre where God has revealed himself. All the children are amazing, lovely and have the heart of God. The entire staff are hard-working people full of God's love and joy.

This is a worthy place to invest your prayers, heart and support. I recommend for you Blessings Hope, for it's a centre where children grow in fertile soil. God bless you as you come to know more about Blessings Hope.

Pastor Samuel, Director:

What a great blessing and honor it is to have such a powerful and God-fearing team! Always I am so blessed to have these people. Surely God connected us together for a powerful reason. Together, we are going to touch many souls which will bring true transformation to our nation, the continent of Africa and the entire world. I do believe and know that our teachers and the entire staff are not here only to work, but to minister. They are people who love God and are always ready and willing to serve the children. Through their great ministry, they have impacted children's lives and shown them a bright future. I am very proud of them, and always they are in my heart and prayers.

Support Staff

Note: See *Meet the Teachers* and read their testimonies in Appendix A at the end of the book.

Part Three

CHALLENGES TO THE DREAM

Chapter Nine

Spiritual and Physical Attacks

*Be self-controlled and alert. Your enemy the devil prowls around
like a roaring lion looking for someone to devour. Resist him,
standing firm in the faith, because you know that your brothers
throughout the world are undergoing the same kind of suffering.*

I Peter 5:8-9

Joyce:

*O*ne of the main challenges for Blessings Hope is spiritual
attack. Satan is not happy about the deep redeeming, healing
love that flows within Blessings Hope and out to the surrounding
communities and neighboring countries where Pastor Samuel ministers. Like any terrorist, Satan strikes back where the greatest number
of people can be affected.

Although Pastor Samuel has seen plenty of attacks through the
years, *my* first experience of it in Africa was in 2013. After the graduation service and Women's Conference, I was to speak to the leaders
who were there for the festivities. I was to give three sessions.

The first session went well, but partway into the second, I was
suddenly burning up! Then the stomach pain began. I had to be taken

to the visitors' sitting room in the first orphans' house. After a hard-boiled egg for protein and a bottle of Sprite, I felt better. But when I tried to walk back to the striped tent where the conference was being held, the pain redoubled its attack. I made it to the outhouse where I honestly cried out to God, "Just let me die right now and go to heaven!" I'm sure I frightened the sweet women waiting by the outhouse to assist me back to the conference.

Meanwhile, Pastor Samuel's father, Bishop Michael Wafula, had come with a van to take me to the hospital in Kitale. I was basically carried to the van where I slumped over onto the back seat, unable to sit up.

But I didn't want to go to the hospital. I'd visited other patients there, and I wasn't so sure it would be helpful. Furthermore, I didn't have the cash that would be required before the doctor would treat me. So I persuaded Bishop Michael to change course and head for Zipporah Kittony's home where we were staying. Carol and Fay had taken the day off to relax and fellowship at home, so I knew they would be there to care for me if I needed it.

However, just ten minutes down the road toward her home, the pain left completely. I was weak but totally pain free! It was as though when I was no longer a speaker at the conference, Satan lost interest and gave me up. I truly believe that it all happened to keep me from bringing an important message of healing to the pastors and leaders.

We didn't know it at the time, but earlier on that same morning, police officers had arrived at Blessings Hope to arrest Pastor Samuel just as he was going into early morning prayer! He had been falsely accused by a jealous neighbor of felling a tree into the man's cornfield and damaging his crops. It was a totally bogus charge as the police discovered when Samuel showed them the unharmed field.

When they tried to arrest him according to the warrant they carried, he simply told them that he had to go to morning prayer and would come to the police station when it was over. They backed off and let him go.

When he arrived at the police station later, the policemen quickly confessed to him in private that they had been bribed by the neighbor and begged him not to tell the chief, or they would lose their jobs. With no evidence of damage, Samuel was released. Humbly and fearfully, the policemen declared that he surely was a man of God.

At other times, the attacks come in the form of sickness.

Samuel:

Dear Mum,

I am so humbled and blessed this morning to let you know that our God is a miraculous God and he hears our prayers. Joel is one of the totally orphaned children at Blessings Hope, and he has been hospitalized for the last six days suffering from four different diseases. He even had a growth in his stomach. He was supposed to undergo surgery according to the report the doctor gave last evening.

Surely I had no peace in my heart. While I prayed through the night, God told me, "It is over, Samuel. I have done my part."

So with the matron and the social worker, I went back to the hospital at about 4:00 this morning. When we arrived, the doctor told us excitedly, "I don't know what has happened with Joel! The growth has disappeared and there is no need for any operation. In fact, Joel was supposed to be transferred this morning to Eldoret General Hospital for more treatment, but there is no need. He has been healed and he is in good condition!"

Joel was discharged that morning, and we brought him home. Wow, this is unbelievable! God really works and hears our prayers! The children in the orphanage had been praying almost all the time, and we are so blessed to see that God has done it!

Another miracle story from Samuel:

Dear Mum,

I am so blessed and humbled to have this great moment and get in touch with you once again, above all to share with you a short testimony about our newborn baby boy, Nehemiah Kibali Strong.

First, I send words of thanks and appreciation to all who helped pay the huge bill which we had in the hospital. May the God of mercy grant you great favor and meet with the needs of your hearts in Jesus' name. I speak words of life into your families, businesses and whatever you may touch. I declare that they are blessed. No weapon formed against you will prosper, in Jesus' name.

And now, for our boy's great testimony:

My wife started complaining of labor pains around 12:00 noon. I took her to Sister Freda's Medical Centre about 1 p.m. By the time we reached there, according to the doctors' examinations we were told that she wouldn't deliver before 9 p.m. So my mum and I decided to go back home and prepare some meal for my wife Sharon and Joyce, one of our friends from Lodwar who was staying at the hospital with her. (Hospitals often don't provide meals.) Around 7:30 p.m., after buying some food and getting ready to go back home to prepare the meal, we received a phone call from Joyce sharing with us that my wife was about to be taken into the theater (operating room), and I was greatly needed to sign the forms. So we returned to the hospital.

When we reached there, I was called into the doctor's office and told that my wife needed to be operated on immediately. If we delayed, the doctor said, we might lose her together with the expected child. I was confused and didn't agree that we might lose them. So I ran out of his office and sat in my vehicle where I stayed for almost two hours, just praying and asking God to release my wife to give birth without an operation. What made me pray for her to deliver without the operation is that the procedure is complicated and the skill needed for it is great, so the possibility of failure is real. Some women have died during this operation.

But I didn't yet get an answer from God. So I went back to the doctor and asked him to release my wife so that I could take her to the government hospital (Kitale District Hospital), since their costs would be lower. So he prepared everything, but before he could give me the forms and his report, he was called into the labor room. Another woman was giving birth, which took him another two hours. By the time he came out, he was sorry for the delay, but still he was asking me not to take my wife to the District Hospital. He insisted that I take more time to think it over before transferring her.

By then it was around 2:00 a.m., but still I told him that I didn't think I could meet with the costs, so he gave me the papers to release us. Even so, I would still have to pay around 4,500 Ksh ($45.00)— which I didn't have—so that she could be released. So I decided to go once again to pray, with my heart full of pain, to see if God would answer my cry.

This time, God gave me the answer! He told me, "Let her go through that process, and you will see my glory."

This voice came to me about three times while I was praying and asking God why he had forsaken me. After realizing that God had answered, I went back in and gave the doctor my consent. He made a call to the theater doctor to come. It took the surgeon almost half an hour to arrive, by which time my wife was prepared and taken into the theater.

I asked the doctors if I could join her and see what would take place. I was allowed, and during the operation, the doctors found that my wife had ruptured. They stood almost a minute without moving, then one of the nurses asked them to just take out the child even if he was dead.

At they took out the child, he started crying! They were so surprised and amazed. "He is alive!! He is alive!!" we all cried. There was great joy and dancing in the room.

One of the doctors told me, "Surely God loves you! If you are not yet saved, this is the time to get saved since you have seen the glory of God!"

I was so surprised to hear such words come out of the doctor's mouth. I replied, "I am saved! In fact I am a pastor!" They told me, "Surely, you are serving a mighty God."

The doctor later told me that he has been practicing medicine for more than 10 years, and during that time, he had never witnessed a child being born alive after such a rupture. He saw the miracle as full of the glory of God. They also discovered that my wife had ruptured three hours before the operation!

So I saw the glory of God just as he had predicted when I was praying. God has done so much for us! I don't know what can now separate me from his love and from serving him. I am filled with the joy of the Lord and will serve in his house the rest of my life! In Jesus' name, Amen!

We are all doing well—my wife Sharon, Ellen, Nehemiah and I.
God is great on our way. We love you and pray that you are blessed.
From your son, Samuel

Samuel and family leaving the hospital

Joyce:

A few weeks later, what appeared to be an infection had developed in the area of her operation. She had been admitted and Samuel wrote for prayer. I alerted everyone to pray. The next day, I received an email from Samuel with great news.

Samuel:

Dear Mum, praise God!

Thank you for your prayers! Yesterday when she was admitted, examined and scanned, it was discovered that she had a growth and needed an operation to remove it.

But through the believers' prayers, God has done something great! This morning the doctor told me that the growth has melted! God is above all!

She is still in the hospital, so please keep on sending your prayers, Mum, and keep asking the believers to join us too. Otherwise I am rushing to the hospital to check on her. I will keep updating you as we keep going on with the prayers. Stay blessed.

From your son, Samuel

(Soon he wrote again.)

Dear Mum, praise Jesus!

I am so thankful for your prayers! May God bless you all mightily for standing in position to pray for my wife. Sharon is doing well, and she will be discharged this afternoon.

I praise God for what he has done. Surely we didn't expect to see such a great testimony! Through the miracle that these people have seen, they are happy to see how faithful the God whom we are serving is!

Joyce:

While God heals many times, there are other times he carries Blessings Hope through deep waters.

An email from Samuel a few months later:

Mum, surely we have been having challenges with sickness in our school. Several children have been admitted to the hospital at various times. It has even reached a point of nearly losing little Elijah! So please keep our school and the centre in your prayers and break all Satan's plans.

It is also very painful to see that we are having to pay such big amounts for the hospital bills. These expenses take funds from what we would normally use for the needs of all the children.

But even so, I know and believe that all these trials are part of the process for us to be equipped. It is my humble prayer request that God may help us persevere as we accomplish our vision and mission for the better future of these children.

Otherwise thank you for everything, Mum. God bless you all.

From your son, Samuel

(In 2016, we were able to secure medical insurance for all children and staff. Praise God!)

Joyce:

Other attacks involve theft. One of my favorite stories of victory is about a solitary goat thief.

In 2013, friends and family here in the States donated money to buy several goats for Blessings Hope to provide milk, especially for the very young children. These dear goats were the delight of the boys who took turns leading them around and showing them off to visitors. I asked Samuel to name them after members of my family. To a Kenyan, naming your animals is very strange (you may eat them someday), but he complied. He even named one after me!

Well, one dark night before we were able to supply the centre with a generator to power a spotlight for security, a thief crept onto the property and tried to steal one of the goats. (Whether it was "Joyce" or not, I don't know.) The night watchman caught him in action and called Pastor Samuel.

Samuel arrived and spoke gently with the thief.

"My friend, why would you want to steal this goat from the children?" he asked.

Overcome with emotion, the man confessed, "I have never stolen anything before, but my children are hungry!"

Samuel then shared with him how God loved him and about the salvation his Son Jesus was offering him. The thief, in tears, accepted that love and salvation and gave his life to Jesus. Samuel gave him food to take home for his children and invited him to come to the Blessings Hope Healing Church on the next Sunday. The man came and brought his family. Praise God!

Chapter Ten

The Testing of Faith

*Now, in all these things we are more than conquerors through him
who loved us. For I am convinced that neither death nor life, neither angels nor demons, neither the present nor the future, nor any
powers, neither height nor depth, nor anything else in all creation
will be able to separate us from the love of God that is in Christ
Jesus our Lord. Romans 8:37-38*

Joyce:

A pastor's faith is probably tested more often than anyone's.
If the enemy can defeat or discourage him over a long
period of time, the enemy can easily take down the entire church or
ministry he leads.

Samuel:

*Mum, I am feeling in my heart to share with you some issues we
are facing at the school. Surely I have learned that the more you
love God, the more you face trials and temptations. This has made
me examine how I am serving God as well as research the experiences of other ministers of the gospel. Sincerely speaking, Mum, I*

have faced a lot which has been trying to test my faith. I have even reached the point of asking God, "Am I really on the right track or have I missed the mark and sinned against you?" His answer has been, "NO my son, you are experiencing a baptism by fire. I want to take you to another level, so persevere."

Some of the challenges are sickness and death that we faced at the school during a malaria outbreak this spring; then rulings by the Ministry of Health and Ministry of Construction (requiring us to tear down and rebuild our cook house a short distance away). Sickness struck our school staff and even the chicks that we have struggled to raise.

Surely it is very painful mum to let you know that around 120 chicks which you, Carol and Ellen and others helped us buy and raise have died. Diseases have popped up in our area killing nearly all chickens. This surprised us as well as the veterinarians. We have never missed vaccinating them throughout the year. We have all the receipts and a stock of vaccines that we have been using, and no one has detected which kind of sickness killed them. We were only two months from being able to enjoy the fruits of our labor. Also it surprised us that all the chickens that we had not yet given the latest round of vaccinations are okay—about 70 in number—so we are truly wondering how these things are happening. Please pray for us to stand strong in the Lord.

But above all, our God will remain our God, and we shall keep loving him more and more.

From your son, Samuel

Joyce:

As I reflect on the many stories of living on the cutting edge between good and evil, I am struck again by the power of grace and forgiveness that keeps Pastor Samuel's heart steadfast and restores his hope time and time again.

In 2015, I sent this email to supporters:

Dear Friends and Family,

As you know, the practice of witchcraft is still strong in Africa. Due to recent spiritual attacks, accidents, thefts and death threats against Pastor Samuel Wafula, I feel an urgency to ask you to stand with me in prayer on his behalf.

I ask you to do what I have done: Put a sticky note on or near your computer to remind you each day to pray for physical and spiritual protection from evil for pastor Samuel, his family, his gospel outreach team, the new churches, the orphans and everyone involved with the Centre, including this ministry. **I love the way Jesus prayed for us in John 17:15, "My prayer is not that you take them out of the world but that you <u>protect them from the evil one</u>." Let's pray the same, in Jesus' name.**

When you sit down to check your emails, pray as the Holy Spirit leads you, please.

Satan's time is short, and he is doing his worst to stop the spread of the gospel and frighten and discourage believers. But he will not prevail if we pray for one another!

Love,

Joyce

Not always are actions driven by witchcraft. Often pride, jealousy or fear propels individuals to act against the school and the church.

While I was enjoying the breeze outside between sessions of the Leaders' Conference in the fall of 2016, Samuel carried a couple of plastic chairs from the church and joined me in the cool of the tree grove by the gazebo. He had a sad story to tell me.

Samuel:

"There is a pastor in the area whose people enjoy visiting Blessings Hope Healing Church from time to time. In fact, many of them enrolled their children in Blessings Hope Educational Centre as day students. But after a while, this pastor became jealous of the success and growth of both our church and the school. He was especially angry that a few of his people eventually joined our fellowship.

"One Sunday a few months ago, this angry pastor stormed into the church during a service and cursed me and the church. He also told the people that I was just luring their children into the school with plans to kill them! Some parents from his church who happened to be there ran out of the service in fright. The next day, many of them removed their children from the school.

"But within a short time, nearly all the parents brought their children back to the school. And now, that church has split apart. There is hardly anyone left in it."

Joyce:

This verse comes to mind: *Like a fluttering sparrow or a darting swallow, an undeserved curse does not come to rest.* Proverbs 26:2 When we are attacked falsely, our hearts can remain at peace.

As Samuel shared this story with me, he showed no glee in the pastor's misery. In fact, he had forgiven the man immediately. *Because the curse was undeserved, it had no power over him.*

Then Samuel told me another story, this time about an unscrupulous principal of a neighboring school.

Samuel:

"Our school has been getting very good reviews for its academic achievement. Everyone knows that it is one of the very best in the region. Of course, much of the credit is due the excellent teachers who have felt the presence of God here, seen the eagerness of the children to learn and have been drawn to teach here. These teachers teach out of love for the children and are very gifted.

"Because our teachers are so good, other schools have tried to entice them away from Blessings Hope with the promise of higher pay. The principal of one of these schools targeted our head teacher and one other who was exceptionally successful with the children. He tried everything possible to get them to leave us and join his school, but they wouldn't do it!

"Shortly after that, the Education Department performed an annual review of that school. It was determined that the school was unfit to have a primary school because the leaders did not put the children's needs ahead of their own interests. So their primary school was shut down! Only their high school remains open."

Joyce:

We both sat in awe of the righteousness of God and how serious he is about integrity. Again, Samuel did not rejoice at their misfortune.

But he knows that when a man's ways are crooked, they will be found out.

Finally, I want to share with you on another subject: how God disarmed my air-tight policy on how to handle donations. Here is an email I wrote last year to my supporters:

Dear friends,

I hope you have all had a moment to read my Thanksgiving email about the "lost" $2,000. In summary, we had sent it to be used for the roof of Samuel's house, but he had sensed God directing him to use it instead to buy the metal sheets for the roof of the church that they had been building on the campus. As you know, God had told Samuel, "If you build my house, I will build yours."

Well, my response was a mixture of consternation and an odd sense that God was doing something bigger than building a house. I came to the conclusion that he was stretching my awareness of how all of our money is his, and it is his right to upset our carefully laid plans. But I still didn't know how I would ask you all to give a second time for a roof for which you thought you had already provided. Never before had money that had been given for a specific purpose been diverted to a different need.

I agonized over it in prayer. Then yesterday, I received "the rest of God's story" in an email from a friend faraway:

Dear Joyce,

I've been a bit behind in tending to "life" so just now read your email. Interestingly, I've checked email several times in the past couple of days but felt like it just wasn't the right time to read your update.

Yesterday, I was balancing out my end-of-year giving and prayerfully decided that I had enough to send you $2,000 for Pastor Samuel. I wasn't thinking of anything in particular to use it for, just that $2,000 was the amount to send.

*As I read your email, I just couldn't help but smile... **in God's economy, nothing is "lost."** So, the check will be in the mail tomorrow!*

Samuel and I continue to observe the rules of integrity in using gifts according to given purposes, but we know now that God has the final word. My heavenly father just wanted me to learn that!

Chapter Eleven

A Steep Learning Curve

And my God will meet all your needs according to his glorious
riches in Christ Jesus. Phil. 4:19

Joyce:

*A*frica often falls victim to the tyranny of the urgent—not
by intent, but by cumulative necessity. In other words,
when they get shillings, they spend them because their children
are hungry—even if the landlord is threatening to throw the family
into the street for back rent. For many people there is never enough
money to save for the future and barely enough for today, so every
need is potentially a crisis that requires help.

This even affects their concept of time. There is an expression
common among visitors to Africa: "We're on 'Africa time.'" No
matter how much planning goes into an event, it never begins or
ends on time—as time is counted in Western minds. There are always
extenuating circumstances: cars break down on the rough roads;
many must travel great distances on foot or by bicycle or motorcycle; many get stuck in taxi vans that endlessly stop along the way
to jam in more people than can conceivably fit by our standards of

comfort. There's no timetable. Many people don't wear watches or cannot afford them. They will get there when they get there.

For both of the above reasons, people live from moment to moment. There is little thought or means to plan ahead as we are able to do in the West.

I now wonder if perhaps the government is trying to change the thinking of the people with all its regulations. For instance, in 2016, the government began requiring all schools, public and private, to buy health insurance for all staff and students. In the past, every illness was a crisis because to be treated in the hospital, one must have cash up front. During malaria season, this was a constant concern for me. The cries for help were many and the costs high.

After a final drive to raise the money needed for insurance, Blessings Hope cruised through the year with all expenses covered whenever illness struck. What a paradigm shift for rural Kenya and Blessings Hope!

The very regulations that had felt like curses raining down upon us over the past two years have proven to be a blessing. At first, I had thought that they were trying to "kill" Blessings Hope Educational Centre and every other struggling grassroots humanitarian endeavor! But now I see that every regulation has made Blessings Hope a more professionally-run enterprise which is also safer for the children and staff.

Government regulations between 2013 and 2016 included: moving the outhouse to another location for health reasons; requiring certified teachers and a government-approved curriculum; enlarging the dorms to sleep just one child to a bed instead of two (which additionally requires more bedding and beds as well); installing a new and better well pump to ensure the safety of the children as they use it for drinking and for washing; requiring the hiring of more teachers and raising wages; replacing the mud cookhouse with a huge dining room and kitchen with high-volume, vented cookers to prevent smoke from being inhaled by kitchen staff as they prepared food; erecting a building just for meeting with visitors, parents and government officials and for teachers to tutor when needed; registering and insuring the school van and making sure the driver is certified and insured as well; and requiring the purchase of health insurance for all children and staff. These are just a few of the costly regulations we have faced and overcome by the grace of God.

We are facing a serious security need at this time. By government order, a concrete security wall must be built to encircle the *entire* compound to protect Blessings Hope from theft and terrorism. A brick wall presently borders about 30% of the compound, leaving a vast area accessible by way of the fields. If attackers advanced now, it would be very difficult for the two watchmen to fend them off.

God has inspired people in the U.S. to give—sometimes at great sacrifice—when each new regulation has been levied in the past. We now pray for God to provide through his people—this time for this vital concrete security wall by the close of 2017.

From the very beginning of Blessings Hope Educational Centre, God has been orchestrating everything, even my growth during hard times. Fundraising can be a relentless tutor in faith, self-discipline and endurance. I'm learning to trust God in ways I never needed to before.

But I do not *enjoy* living by the "tyranny of the urgent." I don't enjoy the fear that sometimes accompanies opening an email from Pastor Samuel that another crisis is upon us and the deadline is fast approaching! However, until the businesses are fully producing the income needed to support Blessings Hope at the level necessary for success and longevity, such tyranny will be unavoidable. By the grace of God, the wise planning that Pastor Samuel is pursuing *will* produce self-sufficiency within a reasonable time. Meanwhile, this all belongs to God. It is his dream, and he has not forgotten us.

Running a school and home for 180 children has exposed all of us to a massive learning curve. Right now we are facing the cold, hard fact that the used van we had purchased in 2012 is no longer adequate. It's a miracle that it has lasted this long and survived all the breakdowns it has had.

We know *now* to avoid, if possible, buying a vehicle that is "used." In Africa, a "used" van has more than likely already been "consumed." In the long run, such a van can cost more in repairs than buying a new one!

In response to the excellent reputation of Blessings Hope Educational Centre, many parents in surrounding villages are enrolling their children as paying day scholars. This is a good source of revenue and very welcome. However, the students must currently be transported to and from school by Blessings Hope's old van that repeatedly breaks down, requiring Samuel to rent a taxi van as well as pay for repairs!

Securing a new (or good-as-new) 32-passenger mini-bus has become an urgent challenge for Blessings Hope. The mini-bus that is needed will cost between $30,000 (used) and $50,000 (new), which sounds to our little ministry like a *million* dollars. But $50,000 is nothing to God and those who listen for his voice. As we pray for another miracle, we believe that God will whisper to just the right people, organizations or foundations that would love to help fund this wonderful vehicle!

A testimony about regulations from Samuel:

Mum, I have a true and living testimony to share with you, and this is the result of prayer. Today I went somewhere just to relax and have my time with God. Around 5 p.m., my wife called me and told me that today we almost lost Rodah, one of our orphans!

Our water pump machine had failed. Rodah and other children were getting water from the wheel manually. It seems that as she was drawing out the water, the wheel became very heavy and she was pulled back into the wheel! The good thing, by the grace of God, is that the wheel was small, so she couldn't pass through it and fall into the well. By the assistance of others, she was saved, although her hand was dislocated. But the medical insurance paid her bill of 15,000Ksh ($150), including the ambulance!

While we were still working on Rodah, we were informed that Winnie, another child, had had an accident while running, and her hand was broken! This second news was like a bomb to me, but I lifted my eyes to the Lord. I told him that I knew he had a way out. Winnie was taken by the school van to the hospital, and right now she has been treated and released to go home. So the children are well and we thank God for His care. Winnie's bills have been covered by the medical insurance too.

So we bless God for everything. I am now seeing the importance of the government's rules. Even if they are very hard to meet, they will be for the best for our children.

From your Son Samuel

Part Four

VICTORIES

Chapter Twelve

Love from Many Directions

The Lord has done great things for us, and we are filled with joy.

Psalms 126:3

Joyce:

Dear friends and family (in spring, 2015):

everal months ago, I described how I respond to the many needs shared with me by Pastor Samuel regarding Blessings Hope: I pray about them and then wait to see if God wants us to be a part of solving the problem. Sometimes he gives me huge joy or a clear vision of why we should respond. However, sometimes I sense nothing, or just have peace that we need not respond. In the latter case, I leave it with the Lord.

*I've often wondered how all the amazing things at Blessings Hope are accomplished that go way **beyond** what we provide. For instance, last Christmas, I received an email from Pastor Samuel expressing his desire to honor 35 widows from Blessings Hope and the community with new clothes and a dinner in his home, as was the custom in Kenya at Christmas. I didn't sense the Lord telling me to do anything about it but trust him. So I didn't share the need with you.*

But I have always wondered if the widows got their new clothes and special dinner. Last week as I was checking Facebook, I went to Samuel's page and began reading the posts. A ways down the page, I came upon a long post he had written not long after Christmas, and I began to cry. Here's "the rest of the story" to encourage you today:

From Samuel:

Greetings to all of my FB friends, and Happy New Year 2016. I bless the name of our living God for giving me this opportunity just to encourage someone who has lost hope in the 11th hour. Just allow me to share a short testimony here, and I believe you will be encouraged and know that our God always works at the last point.

By the beginning of December, people here in Kenya were very busy planning and preparing to welcome friends and family members to join them to celebrate Christmas. One night on my bed, I started to think about how far God has brought us, and I felt in my heart just to be a blessing to the orphans and the local widows. That night I made a covenant with God that on the 25th, we will not go and celebrate in our friends' homes as we usually do. Instead, I will arrange a dinner at my own home so that we can celebrate together with the widows and the orphans who are under our care.

I don't know how people in other countries celebrate Christmas, but here in Kenya, according to our culture, someone will not say that they have enjoyed Christmas unless he or she has eaten well, and above all, is dressed in new clothes. So the next day I told my wife what was in my heart to do and asked her to join me in prayers that we would be able to achieve our goal.

The following day I called the widows' secretary and asked her to give me the measurements of clothes for 35 widows and the sizes *of ten pairs of shoes for the neediest. Also I asked her to pass out a notice that all widows will be my guests on December 25th. We did the budget and it would cost around 120,000 Ksh ($1,200).*

The secretary questioned me, "Pastor Sam, how are you going to raise this money?" I told her that God will provide, so she passed the word and the widows prepared to come.

Now the challenge started. My small business through which I had hoped to raise the funds was closed down. Then one of the needy girls who is under my care was discovered with a growth and required an operation to remove it that would cost around 55,000 Ksh ($550). So I spent almost everything which I had on her needs while the days passed quickly. So I reached the 22nd with nothing in my hand.

The secretary called me, "Pastor Sam, this is the day we need to do the shopping, so can you come over now?" I told her that I would come by tomorrow, without knowing where I was going to get such a large sum.

But in the night around 11 p.m., I received a call from one of my church members who is working with the UN in South Sudan. He told me, "Pastor, it has been almost six months since I have been able to talk with you due to poor means of communication, but I have a gift for you. Just use it however God may direct you."

He gave me a reference number, so the next day I went to the bank and was very surprised to see that he had sent me 150,000 ($1,500)— an amount he had never given before! Immediately we called the widows' secretary and some of the widows' board members and gave them the good news. We were able to buy the clothes and shoes for them, as well as food and soft drinks for the celebration.

I hope you can see the miracle that God did. So I want to encourage you, maybe there is something that you have been praying for and planning, and you have reached a point of giving up. Please, please don't give up. Keep on trusting the Lord. Our God is on the way in the 11th hour. He is so faithful and always ready to accomplish his word. In fact, this is not the first miracle that God Has done for me. There are too many to count, and all have happened at the 11th hour.

God bless you and I wish you all success. Enjoy another wonderful, blessed year, 2016.

Joyce:

In November 2016, Carol and I traveled again to Kenya. This time it was for the Fourth Annual Graduation at Blessings Hope Educational Centre. Having learned how special new dresses were to the widows at Christmas time, Carol and several of her friends had donated about $800 toward providing them. When we arrived, we discovered that the dresses could be made right at the Blessings Hope tailoring shop! All that was needed was the material. The cost would be much less than having to buy them at the ready-made dress shops in town, and the cost would be easily covered by the donations that Carol had brought. Praise God!

Speaking of donations by friends, my thoughts travel back to 2012 and the miraculous outpouring of financial help that occurred during the early years of Blessings Hope. The needs were so great! As explained in an earlier chapter, an educational fund that had been established by Carol's father in memory of her mother paid for the orphans' houses and the classrooms for grades pre-kindergarten through grade 6. But there was much more needed such as a van to transport children and supplies; beds, bedding and mattresses; desks, books, school supplies, uniforms, shoes and socks; cows and goats for milk; seed and fertilizer; and tons of rice, beans and maize. In addition, the government stepped in just as classes were to begin in 2013 and required certified teachers and approved curriculum, neither of which they had yet. These too came at a high price.

So God arranged for miracles that covered every need. I have already recounted some of them, but there are more that stand out in my memory.

Carol is friends with a family with six children. Money is not plentiful in their home, to say the least. But their hearts know no limits when it comes to love and compassion for those who have even less than they. The children have piggy banks in which they save any change that they are given. When they looked at the list of the needs the orphans faced at Blessings Hope, beds captured their attention. They wanted to help supply a bed if they possibly could.

Back then, Blessings Hope bought or built wooden bunk beds that slept two in each bed. So one set of bunk beds would sleep four children. What a deal! The children emptied their piggy banks and produced enough (with a little help from their parents) to purchase one set of bunk beds, giving four orphans a place to sleep in comfort and security!

Over the years, many children have helped: One of my grand-daughters made lemonade and sold it to passersby on a hot, summer day and made $20 to send to Blessings Hope; the youth group from my daughter's church held a spaghetti supper to raise $300 for additional playground equipment; and a friend's children sold their outgrown toys for $30 and donated the proceeds. All gifts count, no matter what the size, and God blesses the givers with joy!

As Blessings Hope opened, there was a desperate need for a school van. I shared the need with supporters, and they began to pray.

Meanwhile, Pastor Samuel tracked down a used van that was in reasonably good condition, and funds began coming in. However, at the time school was to start, we still lacked $3,000 to buy it. Then one day a check for that exact amount arrived in the mail!

Defying all logic, God had spoken about the desperate need for a school van *to a divorced mom who was battling cancer!* Honestly, I would never have expected a struggling cancer patient with no outside support to tackle buying even a bed, much less a van! Accompanying the check was a simple note expressing her joy at being able to complete the purchase of the van for Pastor Samuel and the precious orphans at the school in faraway Kenya. I wept.

It was just a matter of months before she died and went to heaven to be with Jesus. What a legacy of love she left in Kenya! I'll never forget her life and her love for Blessings Hope. Yes, we now need a larger vehicle, but that first van has been a workhorse (albeit now a tired workhorse) for Blessings Hope for four years! That van got us over so many obstacles and performed so many services for the school, the children and for Samuel's far-ranging ministry out into remote villages. Praise God for that lovely van!

Blessings Hope's first van

Just when I thought I had seen more miracles and surprises than I could bear, I was given a precious gift unlike any other I had ever received. One wintry morning in early 2016, Carol arrived at our Tuesday cafe meeting with a pint-sized Mason jar full of coins and currency. Most amazing, however, were the scores of little folded slips of colored paper mixed in with the money. On the slips were notes of encouragement, prayers and scripture verses written whenever God prompted this person to pray for my ministry.

I couldn't imagine who had sent this. Finally, Carol confessed that a friend who wanted to remain anonymous had given it to her to pass on to me. This is a woman who has a painful, incurable disease.

And yet, she thought of me and bore my concerns to the Father even as she was suffering! When she had any extra money, she deposited it in the jar with a note. The jar was packed full!

Slowly I began pulling the slips out one by one, trying to read each aloud to Carol. But I was emotionally overwhelmed and my voice failed. Finally, Carol had to read them aloud to me.

I was so humbled, so moved by this woman's love. Here was a woman whom I had never helped in any way, but whose heart was so open to the Holy Spirit that she would pray and sacrifice for my ministry without ever telling me her name! I deposited the money into my ministry's Blessings Hope account, but I've kept the jar of the notes on my desk. Whenever I need encouragement, I re-read them.

Several months later, there was an anonymous gift of $100 left at the church in an envelope addressed to my ministry. To this day, I don't know who left it for me, but I wonder if it too was from the giver of the jar and the tiny slips of paper.

When the children needed new shoes in 2016, a young mom who teaches music in Pennsylvania wanted to help, but had no resources to send. So she stepped out on a limb and offered a free music theory seminar to the public to benefit the children and provide them with new shoes—and it was a success! What fun it was to look at the pictures Samuel sent of the smiling children donning their new shoes!

When we needed to replace Grace, the milk cow that had died, a donor wrote saying, "If one cow's a good thing, then two will be even better! There's a check in the mail to cover both. God bless you!" When we needed $8,000 to feed the children from January until November when their first harvest would be taken in, donations poured in from personal friends in the U.S., Russia, England and Sweden!

Another donor and friend often knows just when I am in greatest need. Sometimes when the giving has dropped off before there is enough to complete a vital project, she writes to me asking, "How much is still needed?" After I answer, she replies, "The check will be in the mail tomorrow." She gives out of a tender heart that is ever grateful for all the healing Jesus has done in her life. Again, I am in tears as I remember!

In 2016, when the government suddenly said more teachers must be added to the school staff, I sent out a plea for more sponsors. I got a call right away from a young woman who was all excited because she had unexpectedly received a large bonus at work and wanted to give all of it to help us over this financial crisis! That gift especially saved the day for Blessings Hope.

That was also the year that Samuel was offered that unusual opportunity to buy 450 chicks and laying hens from a neighbor who was selling his farm and moving to Norway, but he had no money. Supporters rose up and supplied all the funds to buy the chickens "for the children." The number of chickens in this flock was several times the number that had died in 2014. Furthermore, not only did supporters buy the chickens, they funded the building of a two-story chicken house that was airy and safe for the new egg producers. (More about this later)

I remember when many people helped purchase a motorcycle to make short trips to town for supplies and for Samuel to use to visit church members or go to villages to preach. It really saved money on transportation and filled the gap left whenever the van broke down.

Early on, donors also joyfully donated the funds to buy seven goats that would give quality milk for the youngest orphans, and a donkey and cart to assist with farm chores. Today the children's diets are filled with food from their own fields, milk from their goats and cows, and eggs from their very healthy chickens!

The point is: God loves the children at Blessings Hope and he calls us, his "big" children from around the world, to love them as he does. He provides through us, and we are all thrilled to be part of his plan.

God's dream for them has become ours. And while we are just simple, everyday believers with lives and cares of our own, he enables us *together* to produce miracles of provision that will forever bless and strengthen the faith of children who had been without hope before Samuel found them. It's all marvelous because it's all about God, his heart and his character.

Chapter Thirteen

God Never Forgets

Joyce:

*S*ome days, miracles are commonplace and stop taking us by surprise. Other days, the heavens are silent and we wait and wait.

Then there are the days when God brings into the present moment something prayed for long ago.

Since the beginning of our involvement with Blessings Hope, I had been talking to God about my desire for a unique sport for the children. It would have to be space and cost efficient. At first, I thought it could be track or cross country, but it had to be something that could be contained within the recreation area of the compound. After finding out the price of track shoes and looking realistically at the space that would be available, I ruled that out.

In the spring of 2016, during a lull in my pursuit of this elusive sport, I was with a friend at a cafe where I study and write. We were happily chatting about the children and all the wonderful things God was doing at Blessings Hope. It was quite a spirited conversation.

Across the aisle was a young businessman working on his laptop. But he was also listening to us and finally couldn't contain himself.

"Please forgive me for eavesdropping," he began politely, "but I couldn't help but overhear what you were saying about the orphans' home and school in Kitale, Kenya. It sounds like a wonderful place!"

"It is!" I assured him. "The one thing we are missing is a very special sport that all ages, both boys and girls, could have fun with either individually, as partners or small teams," I added wistfully. "They have a good soccer team, but I can't escape envisioning something that could be enjoyed individually and without needing a great deal of coaching or supervision."

His eyes lit up as he quickly responded, "Have you ever considered competitive or exhibition jumping rope?"

I admitted to him that I had marveled at a demonstration on YouTube a few years ago and then taken some inexpensive jump ropes to Kenya, but since then had forgotten all about it.

He continued, "My roommate and best friend in college went on to found a non-profit organization called 'One World One Rope' and has a team that trains kids in Kenya!" He and I were both getting excited. "The organization is a relatively young one, but it is already training and establishing clubs in many countries. Its roots are in Africa, and its aim is to establish sustainable, independently-run programs around the world, creating a network of youth united in their love for the sport of jumping rope. May I put you in touch with the founder, Michael Brown?"

"Of course! Please do!" I answered without hesitation.

He promptly texted Michael, telling him about Blessings Hope Educational Centre and our interest.

"Michael says to give you his cell phone number and all his contact info and recommended that you check the One World One Rope website to get better acquainted with what can be done in Kenya."

By then, I had moved from excitement to incredulity to utter joy at the prospect of the kids being introduced to this fascinating sport! They were such quick learners and so creative and agile! They would take to it like ducks to water. Even the little ones could do it!

I emailed Michael as soon as I got home, and he referred me to Innocent Nyangori, Co-Chair and team leader of the Jump Rope Association of Kenya, an organization that targets children who have fewer advantages. Innocent lives in Kenya, but he and the team give demonstrations and train children around the world. He is the perfect representative for the Jump Rope Association—humble, joyful, unselfish and visionary. After discussing with me the cost of all the professional beaded ropes that we would need, both single and double Dutch; transportation for the team from Nairobi across Kenya to Kitale and back; and room and board during their visit, we selected tentative dates for the three or four days of training at Blessings Hope when Carol and I would be there in November. The dates cleared with Samuel, so we were on!

As I reflect on how this plan fell into place, I see God's fingerprints all over it. This was very important to him…important to see his children laugh and jump and learn something wonderful and new, and important because it may change the future for Blessings Hope in some way. God thinks of everything and has many purposes that we cannot readily comprehend. And whenever he connects us, his children, to one another for a purpose, it is a divine appointment. In every divine appointment—wherever we are around the world—he is up to something good.

The team of athletes, ranging from 8 years of age to 25, fell in love with the Blessings Hope children, and they with the athletes. Many leaders from other countries, who had just attended the conferences at which I had been speaking, stayed on for the public demonstration and were amazed! Local village children were invited in and several participated in the training. I could see the fulfillment of the vision of Jump Rope Association of Kenya playing out before our eyes: to foster confidence, train leaders and build community. This vision fit well with Samuel's for Blessings Hope as well.

The program was an instant success! I received this email from Innocent after I was back in the States:

Dear Joyce,

My team and I would love to take this special moment to thank you and your entire team for making this successful. Due to your effort and support, we were able to meet these amazing, eager and disciplined children of all ages. Thank you for your warm welcome to BH and taking care of our needs while there.

We were able to work with the kids for three full days. They are fast learners and were able to put together a short show during their closing ceremony. They didn't want us to leave nor did my team want to leave. They can become a very good and competitive jump rope team in the world. Our organization is really eager to keep the sport going, and we would love to support Blessings Hope with any help they may need from us. I see the BH jump rope team going far.

Whenever you like, I can put you in touch with Jump Rope Clubs in the U.S. that might enjoy helping you with additional ropes and funds to allow for further training at Blessings Hope and Kitale.

To Pastor Samuel, our thanks for his hospitality. He is surely a very good guy. We had a discussion with him about the way forward which I think he is going to share with you. If we wish the team or sport to grow, we will need to visit the team occasionally to ensure its progress.

Our main goal is to be able to do quarterly jump rope camps and competitions in both Nairobi and Kitale. I hope to do a number of camps in Kitale to prepare them before having them come to Nairobi for the holiday camps.

The kids in the community liked the sport as well and wish to continue with it. We are in touch with them both on the phone and through other social media. We hope this relationship progresses well and benefits them too.

We do look forward to working with you again. Once again we thank you very much for your support and hospitality. May the almighty God bless you.

As usual if there is anything we can do for you, don't hesitate to contact us.

Sincerely,
Innocent Nyangori
Jump Rope Association of Kenya

Even little ones can learn to swing Double Dutch ropes!

Children jumping everywhere!

The teachers love it too!

During all the years of asking God about a special sport for the children, our heavenly Father had a plan in mind that he would activate at the perfect moment in a way that would totally delight us! What brings tears to my eyes is remembering that he never forgets the pure cries of our hearts for good things, especially for others.

The book of Hebrews speaks to me. It speaks to me of persever-
ance and endurance. It speaks of the character and holiness of God, and
the authenticity of Jesus Christ as His son, our savior and high priest.

Most of all, it speaks to me of faith: the confidence that what we
hope for, promised by God, will actually happen. It gives me assur-
ance about things I cannot see but that he has placed in my heart as
a reality. I've been living in the book of Hebrews lately.

Blessings Hope has arisen from nothing but faith and reflects the
glory of God.

But there have been tough times. Besides unexpected illnesses
and the machinations of the enemy, the government's requirements
at times burdened and sapped our courage to carry through on the
call. The laws came relentlessly, draining us of resources that we
would rather have used for direct ministry to the children for their
care and their education, and to the staff for their hard work, sacrifice
and personal survival. We had to constantly step back and regain our
bearings. *Did God call us to do this? Do we believe that he is strong
enough, loving enough to work all things—even government inter-
vention —to the good of Blessings Hope without destroying it?* For
me, fundraising became a constant concern, and prayer in the woods
alone, a necessity for my spiritual life and peace.

This morning, I had an epiphany of sorts when I read Hebrews
2:11. In NIV it reads, "Both the one who makes men holy and those
who are made holy are of the same family. So Jesus is not ashamed
to call them brothers." Jesus goes on to say to God, "I will declare
your name to my brothers; In the presence of the congregation I will

sing your praises," and further down he says, "Here am I, and the children God has given me."

(In the NLT translation, Jesus says "brothers *and sisters*" both times. That blesses me because I know it is true.)

The point struck me gently: *Jesus stands with us before the Father.* He declares God's name to us and then he stands and worships the Father side by side with us.

He is standing with us before the Father whether during trials and hardship while we wait for the results of his intercession, or when the heavens open and blessings flow down without limit. He weeps with us, and he laughs with us. He is compassion and joy personified.

This is GOOD! What a Savior we have! How above anything we could imagine is he! Yet he *describes* himself and his heart so that we WILL imagine what he's like and be more intimate with him. He lets us "see" him and feel his presence.

Am I crazy? Or is this not the simplest understanding of all?

When something wonderful or just plain sweet happens, it is as though he lands kisses on our foreheads or gives us long hugs. As I read Hebrews, I remember the kisses and hugs God has given me, especially those that reinforce his call to serve Blessings Hope.

God shares his dreams with us. He remembers our needs and provides. He hears our cries and acts—even arranging a meeting in a café for me with someone who just happened to be in our town on business and could put me in touch with just the right person to introduce me to the Jump Rope Association of Kenya! He loves us, his earthly children even as he loves his own Son. Nothing good will he withhold from us. We can trust him with all we are and all we have as we face the future—in the land of Kenya or wherever he leads us.

Chapter Fourteen

A Dream That Will Endure!

Blessed are all who fear the LORD, who walk in his ways. You will
eat the fruit of your labor; blessings and prosperity will be yours.

Ps. 128:1-2

Joyce:

*J*ust as soon as the initial parcel of land was purchased and the orphans moved into the first house back in late 2012, Samuel began canvassing directors of successful orphanages with schools to glean insight regarding businesses that would work well for Blessings Hope. We knew that Blessings Hope would grow and the needs would quickly outstrip donations, so from the very beginning, the goal was self sufficiency.

The first idea was logging up on Mt. Elgon. All that would be required was a chain saw, permits and transport. It seemed smart at first, but as we thought it through, we found potential problems of safety and unexpected costs.

One of the best interviews he had was with Bishop Ben, a director who uses tractors as their main source of income. He started with one to do their own plowing, and then rented out the tractor (with a driver) to farmers around who had no such equipment. It really caught on, and now he has two tractors that support several orphanages and schools across the country, with more than 3,000 orphans in primary schools, high schools and universities! This sounded like a winning plan to us.

So we launched the fundraising drive for the "Tractor Project" and people gave generously. It took time, and we had to scale down the size of the tractor we were hoping to buy, but Samuel found a tough, mid-range tractor and plow that could hold its own in any field! The first year, it ran constantly during plowing season and was very lucrative, even though they got a late start in the season while waiting for the money to be donated.

The second year brought an exciting opportunity. I'll let Samuel tell you about it via an email I received from him back then.

Tractor and plow

Samuel:

Dear Mum,

I have connected with the manager of Mumiasi Sugar Company which is giving out six-month contracts for private tractors, some to plow while others transport sugarcane from the field to the company. So I have just worked on several temp jobs in Mumiasi and have been able to raise $1,230 to apply and to finish the paperwork to complete the process. The only remaining hurdle is comprehensive insurance. You know the insurance which we currently have on the tractor is third party, so we are supposed to raise 162,000 Ksh ($1,620) <u>by tomorrow evening</u> so that by Saturday, we can take the tractor to the company, and by Monday it can start the work.

So let us believe in God for this last miracle. Once we are approved, we shall be earning not less than 350,000 Ksh ($3,500) per month! The sugar cane company will be responsible for servicing the tractor and paying our driver and the contractor. So it's some-thing which we shall be having a good income from as we wait for the plowing season to begin back in Kitale.

Otherwise, I look forward to sharing with you much as God leads. But all in all, just know that you are in our hearts and prayers.

From your son, Samuel

Joyce:

Between Friday and Saturday, God blessed us with the money needed for the comprehensive insurance!

Received the next day from Samuel:

Dear Mum, surely I am rolling with tears to see what God is doing. I didn't expect to hear from you this great miracle that God has done in the short time since I shared with you concerning the tractor and the contract deal. May God receive all the glory, honor and praise in the name of Jesus of Nazareth, amen. Mum, I really don't know what I can say about how you and your ministry partners have impacted our lives, but God who sees in secret places will reward you all greatly.

Thanks for also standing with my wife in prayers for safe travel here. She arrived very well, and we have completed everything. Even right now we are in a vehicle heading back home. We were able to pay for the insurance and complete everything. All that remains now is just to sign the contract on Monday, then our machine will start the work. We are so encouraged! We do believe that before the tractor returns to start our own plowing season next spring, we shall be able to earn a good amount which will help us to continue developing Blessings Hope.

From your son, Samuel

More from Samuel:

I want to explain to you about how the sewing and metal working businesses we started in 2015 have developed into a wonderful outreach into the community. This outreach is now called Blessings Hope Training Institute.

Blessings Hope Training Institute was birthed from the heart of God, and it's the little sister of Blessings Hope Educational Centre. Our institute was officially launched in January 2016. The target or vision of our institute is to give skills and offer training to the community, which will lead to self-reliance and the elimination of poverty.

Most people who are benefiting from our institute are teenage mothers, young men who dropped out of school due to the lack of school fees, men and women who had no chance to go to school, widows and many others. Our institute offers training in tailoring, welding, catering, weaving and hair dressing. We are looking forward to offering more things such as secretarial skills and training for Early Childhood Development teachers in the future.

Since its launch, Blessings Hope Training Institute has given great service to the community, brought healing to wounded hearts and inspired hope for a bright future.

This institute/polytechnic has truly changed the atmosphere of our community, and it has created employment as well as generated income for our school and the ministry at large. We thank God because of our partners Mum Joyce and Sister Carol and all supporters for their generous gifts.

Joyce:

Another wonderful source of revenue is, of course, the chicken project. As I shared earlier, Samuel's first venture in raising chickens had been very discouraging when most of the 120 chickens (raised from chicks and finally ready to be productive) died of a strange disease in 2014. Samuel was so heartbroken that he said he never wanted to try raising chickens again! They just seemed too fragile and costly in the long run.

But the chance in 2016 to buy over 400 very healthy and productive chickens from the neighbor who was moving to Norway was irresistible. The fact that Samuel's farm manager had been specially trained in raising poultry was a bonus. The only problem was that there were only three days between learning of the chickens and when they had to be paid for and transferred to Blessings Hope.

It was quite a weekend for Samuel. Blessings Hope was able to get the 300 Samuel originally wanted plus 150 more that were offered to him at the last minute because another purchaser reneged on his promise to buy them. (I really had to scramble to get the word out to supporters and forward all the donations quickly to Samuel.)

Excitement was running high on the campus. They would not only have many more eggs to eat for protein each week, but lots of eggs to sell at the surrounding markets and in Kitale.

As the story unfolded, I just had to laugh while imagining Blessings Hope's farm manager struggling to suddenly accommodate so many chickens at once with no building prepared! Since Blessings Hope hadn't had time to build even a temporary shelter, the farm workers tried to stuff them all into one of the polytechnic shops!

In Samuel's words at the time: "Truly Mum, we don't have the house to keep them in, so right now we are using one room of one of our shops. But we have been advised by our farm manager that it's not safe, because these chickens, they need a lot of air, and this room does not have enough ventilation. Also this shop is next to the road where there are a lot of motorbikes passing by. There is also the children's noise during break time, and these chickens, they are very sensitive and they don't want noise.

"So this morning we were discussing the problem with our farm manager and we saw that they will be safe if we can build a large chicken house. It must be well ventilated, in a quiet place, perhaps alongside my house, for about $2,000. So Mum, this is another miracle for which we need God to intervene.

"So please stand with us in prayer to see what God will do, so that we can have a secure place for these chickens. We have invested a lot, although it's a very profitable project. From the eggs that we started to sell yesterday, we shall have money to buy chicken feed as well as some to put aside. We are going also to open a chicken account at the bank so that by the end of the month, we can see what our earning potential is and how much we could divide between expenses and savings for our vision of expanding our project to 1,000 chickens. We want to be the best seller of eggs in Kitale town and the entire region!"

As I shared in Chapter Twelve, supporters pulled through again for the vision. The two-story chicken house isn't the fanciest coop in the world, but it is well-ventilated, naturally well-lit and has plenty of room for them to move about. There is an area for pullets, another for layers and a third for those molting. I saw the chickens last month while we were there and can testify to their good health and happiness.

Letter from Joyce in 2016:

Dear friends and family,

Last night, I was looking back and considering the great changes that have taken place at Blessings Hope since 2012:

Four years ago, when Blessings Hope was founded, we raised $8,000 for food to get them through to their first harvest. This year, with more land under cultivation, cows and goats for milk and lots of chickens for eggs, they've not needed any help at all for food!

Four years ago, we had to pay a tailor in town to make the children's uniforms. Two years ago, supporters donated funds for two sewing machines and fabric to Blessings Hope to begin their own tailoring shop. This year, the children are wearing brand-new, redesigned uniforms which have been produced in their own shop!

Four years ago, we raised the money for wooden beds. This year, they are sleeping in strong, handsome metal frame beds designed and made in their own metal-working shop!

Two years ago, we helped them install electricity. This year, they are paying their own electric bills.

For three years, we helped them pay the medical bills of several children as well as Samuel's wife when she experienced the dangerous delivery of her son. This year, we helped secure medical insurance for the children and staff, and we have sent no money since for children's medical emergencies!

These are just a few of the ways that God has blessed them through our giving and how effectively they have used it to move quickly toward self-sustainability, long-term security for the children and outreach to the community.

By grace,

Joyce

The Orphan and Teacher Sponsorship Programs, the Scholarship Fund and the Emergency Operating Fund play important roles in the smooth operation of Blessings Hope and will be needed in varying degrees for several years to come. There will still be emergency needs and still something new to build, but gradually the businesses at Blessings Hope will grow and begin covering each need—even the need for an $18,000 concrete block wall around the entire compound! The day of self-sustainability *will* arrive.

I am deeply grateful to all who dream with Samuel and continue supporting Blessings Hope at every turn. Let's look back over these four short years with enormous gratitude to God for the privilege of helping rescue, heal and educate hundreds of children who otherwise would have had no home, no family and no hope. Let's also look forward to the miracles God will surely perform through their lives in the years to come.

Everyone at Blessings Hope — right down to the night watchmen, cooks, matrons, field hands and the dear farm manager who had to create housing for 450 chickens with less than three day's notice — is grateful that friends in the U.S. have believed in what they are doing for the orphans and widows and have supported them. I believe that our "band of believers" will grow into an army of men and women whose greatest joy is making "holy dreams" come true.

And now I thank God that he is "able to make all grace abound to *you*, so that in all things at all times, having all that *you* need, *you* will abound in every good work. As it is written: 'He has scattered abroad his gifts to the poor; his righteousness endures forever.'"

May hope continue rising in Kenya and spread around the world!

Chapter Fifteen

Dreams for the Next Generation

And the Lord said, "Write the vision, and make it plain upon tablets, that he may run that readeth it. For the vision is yet for an appointed time, but at the end it shall speak, and not lie: though it tarry, wait for it; because it will surely come; it will not tarry."

Habakkuk 2: 2-3 (KJV)

Samuel:

*A*lways I am so blessed as I read Habakkuk, for everything that we are seeing today at Blessings Hope has been based on this book. If God has done all this, why can he not do the rest? I strongly believe in him, since he's the same God who has been working since the days of Abraham. He's the same God who is working in our generation too, and he's the same God who will be working in the upcoming generations. He's the same yesterday, today, tomorrow and forever. So I have no doubt in him. My financial challenge of today cannot determine my destiny and the fulfillment of the vision and the dream which God has laid in my heart.

My heart is packed full of **BIG** goals as I look forward to the fulfillment of the dream for this and upcoming generations. After God opens the way for establishing our Junior High School in 2017, we will begin adding a full day and boarding High School in 2018, two classes at a time. It is our goal that all the children from Blessings Hope and those whom we are supporting from different communities across Africa—once they successfully conclude their last primary examinations in November 2018—will be able to join our High School and proceed with their studies right here.

Also, by 2024 we are looking forward to setting up our own university. This will provide an excellent education for those children who have done well in their high school studies—both from Blessings Hope High School and from poor communities across the continent. We pray that they will join us and study so that they can accomplish their dreams too.

This is just part of what God has put in my heart and which I am looking forward to accomplishing. It is my prayer and the desire of my heart for God to show me the right people with great hearts and vision whom we can mentor, so that they can also move with this vision and pass it on to other generations.

If God is speaking to you and you are willing to stand with us in this work, please get in contact with our dear Mum Joyce. She will show you how you can best partner with us to build the Body of Christ and bring hope and a bright future to all generations through Blessings Hope Educational Centre.

Thank you from us all, and God bless you.

Thank you and "thumbs up"!

Epilogue

Is anything too hard for the LORD?

Genesis 18:14

Joyce:

*G*od delights in doing the impossible.

He directs Moses to lead the Israelites on an escape route from Egypt that takes them to the banks of the Red Sea—a river they can't cross.

He asks Noah to build a boat of deliverance to float —on oceans of water that don't yet exist.

He commissions Gideon to face the vast armies of the Midianites— with only 300 men and trumpets, jars and torches.

In every case, the end of the story brings redemption for God's children and hope for the world. In every case, the Holy Spirit first comes upon those who are willing to obey the God who created all things but whom no one can see. None has the resources. None obeys for fame. All pay a personal price. All are worshipers. All are willing to dream with God.

All are passionate.

In Western culture, passion means the fire of human love. The passion Jesus models for us is bound up in a love that is willing to suffer for the sake of others who haven't earned it and may never return it. *His* passion by nature overcomes every obstacle that arises between us and the fulfillment of every promise he has ever made.

I've watched Samuel. I've come to know and trust his heart. From opposite sides of the globe, we've charged together to the edge of the Red Sea; we've prayed for the heavens to open and pour down oceans of provisions to carry Blessings Hope above mountainous waves; and we've been accompanied by stalwart soldiers who aren't afraid of the bigness of the "holy dream" or ashamed to carry the torches and blow the trumpets with us, and who are willing to share great risk and serve with enormous courage.

Samuel knows God, his Word and his ways. *He leads with passion—but also with grace.* This grace involves forgiving others freely in an instant and remembering that without the forgiveness that he received from God's son at Calvary, he'd be without hope as well.

This humility of Samuel's is lived out honestly and unselfconsciously before everyone. This humility now permeates Blessings Hope Educational Centre and is sweetly glorious.

So now I bless Samuel as Jabez prayed to be blessed in I Chronicles 4:9-10:

> *Oh LORD, bless Samuel and enlarge his influence and territory for your glory! Keep your hand steadfastly upon him, guiding him in righteousness. Keep him far away from harm and evil so that his heart remains pure and his ministry brings healing and deliverance to others without regret. Honor him, O LORD, as you did Jabez, so that your dream, carried in Samuel's heart, will bring you honor forever. Amen.*

Appendixes

Appendix A

Meet the Teachers

*Train a child in the way he should go, and when he is old
he will not turn from it.* Pr. 22:6

Teachers in 2017. Seated from left: Madam Margret, Saida, Mercy, Madam Jully.
Standing from left: Mr. Matthew, Dorcus, Madam Margret Njeri, Mr. John, Mr.
Peter, Mr Kenani. Absent from picture: Madam Judith, Ghainet, Chebet,
and Madam Pricilla

Joyce:

*I*t's my pleasure to invite the administrator and teachers to introduce themselves and share their hearts and observations with us. Try to imagine their clear, soft voices and delightful British-flavored Kenyan accents as they speak.

Madam Judith Otiambo, Administrator and Teacher:

I am so grateful to be part of this great, growing and developing Centre. The teaching at Blessings Hope is in accordance with the Kenyan primary teaching curriculum. The teachers are trained and very competent. Because of their effort and commitment, the school is ranked among the top schools in Kenya. The pupils are eager to know and learn new things, even in their co-curricular activities. They are very competitive, with any below-average student improving daily.

The environment at Blessings Hope is very conducive for stability and learning new things for anyone who is open minded. Spiritually, I have personally grown. I am able to learn new things due to the God-centered programs held on the grounds. The Thursday lunch hour meetings are eye opening to me as I learn of spiritual things and am encouraged. Director Pastor Samuel's leadership style is wonderful. It is giving each one of us a chance to develop and bring into the system/department what we know through incorporating our skills and talents. May God bless this work, and thanks to all who are partnering with us.

Peter Simiyu, Head Teacher and Teacher of Grades 4, 5 & 6 Mathematics and Kiswahili:

I trained at Nabongo Teachers Training College and have been teaching since 2010. Why did I take a position at Blessings Hope? One day as I was passing in the area, I heard about how this school was helping the helpless, and it touched my heart. I applied and was accepted.

I was impressed immediately by the comprehensive oversight and assistance that the Administrator gives to the teaching staff. But most of all, I love being with the children. It gives such high meaning to teaching when you are helping those who could never have helped themselves in this world. I also love finding where they are having problems and then how to assist and encourage them.

The teaching of Blessings Hope is very good. The students are very quick learners. We encourage them from the beginning by telling them, "This is your chance to use what you are being given and then to spend your life using it to help others."

The teachers are hardworking, self-motivated and committed to their work. They are ready to help the pupils and have good relationships with them. I am now the Head Teacher, and all of my staff are professionally trained, thus making the performance of the school to be of high quality.

I thank God for the great grace that He has given me to have the skills, knowledge and experience to deal with pupils with different attitudes and backgrounds. Above all, I have gained spiritual knowledge through the lunch hour prayers that we always have on Thursdays. Blessings Hope is on Christian-oriented ground, thus making it conducive ground for excellence.

The leadership of Blessings Hope is also good. Duties have been delegated to every department. The heads of the departments are performing their duties with excellence. I am very proud of this place. I also praise God because of my Director Pastor Samuel, our dear Mum Joyce Strong and the entire working staff. They are people intent on serving the needy with great hearts of love. May God bless them all.

Saida Asman Wekulo, Early Childhood Development (Pre-school) Teacher:

I teach in these three areas:
1. The Baby Class
2. The Nursery
3. The Pre-school Unit

As a professional, I love my job, especially when handling these small children. When the children are hurting or lonely, I simply am friendly and gentle with them. I find out the problem, encourage them and then help change their attitude. In times of sorrow, we share a word from God, praise together and pray together.

I love to help these little ones grow socially and spiritually. Before coming here, I had struggled. I saw the need to touch children spiritually and wanted to help them, but I discovered that there is no better place for them to be healed and be given hope and a future than here.

We help the children express themselves and socialize through singing and dancing. There's an "organized freedom" in this place.

Lunch hour prayer builds me up spiritually. My desire is for Blessings Hope to prosper and be a spiritual ground for pupils, teachers and the community. May God bless my Director Pastor Sam and the entire team of Joyce Strong Ministries. We love you all and appreciate your great support.

Ghainet Wamalwa, Early Childhood Development (Preschool) Teacher:

My first teaching position was at the Tumain Academy. Then I heard about Blessings Hope Educational Centre through a friend. When I visited here, the teachers welcomed me and were very interesting. When I began teaching, the children were happy to see me.

I love teaching here because the pupils are active and freely interact with us and each other. They show their talents freely and they can ask anything they feel like asking.

I love Blessings Hope because it makes me continue to grow up spiritually and socially. I love our Director Samuel because he is a God-fearing man, and he involves God in all he does.

Mum Joyce Strong and all our supporters, may the Lord continue being with you and meet the vision that you have for Blessings Hope. Through your support and prayers, we are able to feed and raise our children. May God's grace be with you and all who are partnering with us. Have a blessed day!

Margret Atieno Odour, Teacher:

I have been a teacher for three years now. My training gave me the knowledge and skills on how to handle kids with different abilities. This taught me how to develop the child holistically — spiritually, mentally and physically. I teach Class 2 CRE and English; Class 5 Science; Class 6 English.

Teaching is a calling, thus I love my job very much. I love instilling knowledge and developing a Kenyan who will be useful in the world of tomorrow. Blessings Hope Educational Centre is a school of excellence and the place to be. I love my Director and the entire staff. I am one of the new teachers and am more than ready to work with BHEC to see that we have achieved our goals and vision. I know that this school is going to be the leading school in our region and the entire land of Kenya.

Mr. John Wekesa, Grades 4, 5 & 6 Teacher:

I graduated from Kyambogo University, Kampala, Uganda. As a teacher I strive to help my children become self-reliant academically and productive in society.

I love the children because teaching is in my heart. It is a joy to see how they give careful attention to the lessons I teach them. I thank God for BHEC. It's really a "blessings centre." I see that it is a wonderful up-and-coming school with a lot of success. In the future, we are going to produce a great nation. Thank you for your support and prayers.

Chebet Rehemah Naibei, Standards 1, 2 & 3 Teacher:

I like teaching because the children love sharing and using their talents to reach their goals and objectives.

Blessings Hope has really changed my life spiritually and mentally. We appreciate our Director Pastor Sam and you all for the support you are giving to us, the orphans and to the community. We really pray for you as you touch lives around the world. May God continue to give you his favor.

Mercy Mutoro, Teacher:

During the time I have had the opportunity to work with BHEC, I have learned a lot that has really inspired my life. Here I get to help provide a good environment and be a suitable example.

There is good interaction between the school and the community around us. The children are well disciplined and high achievers, and Blessings Hope is a good place.

Blessings Hope is a developmental school; it is a performing school and is non-tribal, since it accepts and embraces every tribe. Also, it is a religious school.

The Director is a helpful and hardworking man, loving and caring, God-fearing and persevering.

Mum Joyce, you are loving and kind, someone who is God-fearing, trustworthy, just and loyal. We love you and appreciate you and your team for your great support and prayers.

Kenani Wabwile Wafula, Grades 4, 5 & 6 Teacher:

I was trained at Nabongo Teachers Training where I acquired the skills and knowledge necessary to handle learners with various abilities. The skills have made me able to develop the learners spiritually, mentally and academically.

I love the teaching profession because it makes me learn more and trains me how to reach learners with different abilities. I teach with passion because I like seeing improvement. I want these children to be useful members in their society and nation.

BHEC is a centre with an excellent and conducive environment for academic activities. It is the perfect place to be and work passionately. May God bless my Director Pastor Samuel for the hard work and great commitment that he has, and my sponsor for your support of me in this wonderful place. God bless you.

Dorcus Njeri, Teacher:

I trained at Egoji Teachers College and teach the following classes:
    Grade 4 Science, SST, CRE
    Grade 5 CRE
    Grade 6 Science

I enjoy teaching because to me it's a calling not just a profession. I enjoy nurturing the pupils' talents and imparting knowledge to them so that they will grow to be productive people in society.

BHEC is the best place for working because it is built on a Christian foundation. Although I am new on these grounds, what I have learned is really amazing. My Director Pastor Sam is a man with a big heart for God. He is someone who is very humble, loving and hard working. During the time I have been here, my heart has been full of joy because it was my yearning to work in a place full of joy and peace. May God bless Joyce Strong and the team. I also thank my sponsor with all my heart.

Madam Pricilla Nafula, ECDE and Grades 1 & 2 Teacher:

I teach math, English, science and Kiswahili.

I love teaching because it is my profession. But it is also my calling. I am also a parent, and I would like my family to be blessed through fellowship with these children.

The children are open and lively, and this helps me see what they will be like in the future. As I learn their backgrounds, I learn how to handle each to help them learn.

I like how BHEC develops teachers. Being on these grounds, I have come to know the reasons why one should be a born again Christian and serve the needy children and the community at large. The rules and regulations have made me love my job more and more. The motivation from our Director has helped me improve my standard of living and it has also made me to be more open before people, knowing how to stay and have peace with people.

I thank God because of Joyce Strong Ministries. You are wonderful people of whom we are very proud. Thank you for your support in all ways. We love you and pray for you all.

Matthew Manuka S. Muresia, Standards 2, 3, 5 Teacher:

I teach the following classes: Social Studies, Kiswahili and Mathematics. To the pupils in the entire institution, I give assistance to those with any social or academic problems. I identify pupils with talents in various fields as well.

Teaching has been in my blood for many years. So it is automatic that I love being in the field. I wish for the success of BHEC for the betterment of both the child and the community at large.

Madam Jully Wafula, Standards 1, 2, 3 Teacher:

I teach Kiswahili, Mathematics, English, Science and CRE.

Being a teacher, I understand and teach pupils with different histories, making friendships and handling them as my small siblings, helping them to achieve their goals. Teaching is an ability, and it's a call from God. I love my work as a teacher and I want to go further with these children.

BHEC is an admirable and God-fearing centre. This is a place of disciplined and hard-working staff. I love my Director Pastor Sam. He is a humble man of God with a heart for serving all. May God bless Joyce Strong Ministries for partnering with us. We love you all are are praying for you all the time. May God continue to grant us all his grace as we take these children from one level to another. Special thanks and love go to my sponsor. Thank you!

Mercy Jepkoech, Teacher:

I like teaching pupils and do it wholeheartedly, putting all my efforts into ensuring that the children achieve their social, moral and upright behaviors in order to be dependable people in the upcoming generation. I am proud to be a member of the Blessings Hope community, which is a family that nurtures children in every way.

The Director is focused and depends on God in all his endeavors. His words of encouragement and the prayers of our supporters keep the fire burning. Remember that you all are making a great difference to the lives of many pupils. We are all called to be here. God bless you!

Samuel:

I am so happy! Surely I see what God has done. Right now by the grace of God through the support of our dear Mum Joyce alongside her husband Jim, Sister Carol and her husband Don and the entire team of Joyce Strong Ministries, we have been able to establish and grow Blessings Hope Educational Centre. Our school blesses our community and more than 300 children from across our country and even Uganda! I am so grateful to God for preparing all these teachers, the support staff and me to serve and bring hope to the hopeless. We are focused and looking for great things to happen to transform lives and strengthen our communities in the future. In the name of Jesus Christ of Nazareth, amen.

Appendix B

Blessings Given by Joyce Strong

The Blessing Spoken over Samuel Wafula
October 26, 2013

amuel, God is pleased with you. You are a man who has taken refuge in the integrity of God. As a result, you can say along with David in Psalm 41:12, "In my integrity, you uphold me and set me in your presence forever." Because you trust in God and are grateful for each breath, he has entrusted much responsibility to you. Your humility and childlike faith will continue to guide you through the continuing challenges of leadership and ministry.

Samuel, you are like the Prophet Samuel of old who said, "Here am I," whenever he heard God call his name. I believe that even as a child, you too, could hear God's voice. And because you have obeyed him each step of the way, innocence, excellence, compassion and justice have put down deep roots in your life.

Because you trust unswervingly in God alone, he blesses your ways. Because you know that God's ears are attentive to your cry, He answers even before you call. His love is more precious to you than life. You radiate hope—hope in a God who will not disappoint you.

I pray, Samuel, that you will be a tree planted by the water that bears fruit in its season. May your roots be healthy and strong forever, even when the winds of adversity blow hard. Continue to be truthful with others, as well as yourself. Continue to be the same in private as you are in public. As Titus 2:7-8 says, "In everything set an example by doing what is good. In your teaching show integrity, seriousness and soundness of speech that cannot be condemned, so that those who oppose you may be ashamed because they have nothing bad to say about you or the ministry of Jesus Christ."

May you walk securely in Christ all the days of your life and leave an inheritance of obedience, integrity and love. May that inheritance protect and guide all you lead, including the hundreds of children who will pass through Blessings Hope. May it bless and influence all to whom you give the Gospel of redemption and reconciliation. I pray that integrity will grow and shine through the Body of Christ in Kenya because of the influence of the lives God has touched through you and your ministry.

I commit to do battle in the spirit for you in the days ahead. I commit to pray for your safety and success. I thank God for your childlike faith that says, "Here am I," whenever God calls, even to pursue seemingly impossible tasks. May we meet in heaven where Jesus will say to you, "Well done, good and faithful servant. Enter into my rest."

The Message to the Graduating Class and Teachers at Blessings Hope Educational Centre November, 2014

Congratulations, children! You have studied faithfully, listened to your teachers, and done your best. You are each a beautiful gift of God and a joy to all who know you. But best of all, you are a joy to Jesus!

And now, I would like to pray for you:

Dear Lord, thank you for creating these precious children. They are each unique, gifted and dear to you. I ask you to pour blessings of good health and joy upon their lives. I pray that they will continue to learn and grow in wisdom, and then use that wisdom to bless others. Most of all, I pray that their love for you will increase each day and they will serve you all the days of their lives. In Jesus' precious name, Amen

Now, like Joshua and Esther, be strong and courageous! And like King David and Mary of Bethany, worship the Lord with all your hearts. Finally, like Moses and Jesus' mother Mary, don't be surprised if God has very unusual plans for your life that can change the world!

Teachers, I congratulate you most of all! You have helped shape these young lives each day to bring honor to the Lord and be a blessing to each other and the world. They will look back many times in their lives to the great and beautiful influence you had upon them and the gracious role models that you have been to them. Thank you for filling the classrooms with hope, good character, and the love of God. Thank you for your faithfulness and courage!

And so: *Let us not become weary in doing good, for at the proper time we will reap a harvest if we do not give up.* Gal. 6:9

To Pastor Samuel, staff, friends and family, I leave these words from Philippians 4:4-7: *Rejoice in the Lord always, I will say it again: Rejoice! Let your gentleness be evident to all. The Lord is near. Do not be anxious about anything, but in everything, by prayer and petition, with thanksgiving, present your requests to God. And the peace of God, which transcends all understanding, will guard your hearts and your minds in Christ Jesus.*

The Blessing Spoken over Sharon Wafula At the Women's Conference On November 6, 2015

Sharon, you are precious to God. Your peaceful, quiet heart ministers to me deeply. You are like Mary, the mother of Jesus, who when the angel Gabriel gave her the news of the seemingly impossible thing that would happen to her, she said, *"Let it be unto me as you have said."* You are also like her in that you carry God's mysteries and the questions you have in your heart. There is much more happening in your soul and spirit than others can imagine. You bear much in silence, choosing to trust the unknowable to your God.

Because you are faithful, God holds you close and your husband trusts and honors you. You may be fragile, but you are courageous and steadfast. Your childlike faith blesses your husband, and he delights in your presence. You bring him honor by your faithfulness.

I pray, Sharon, that the Lord will bless you beyond your imagination, even though you ask for little. He will also give you the strength you think you lack, and the wisdom that you need to guard your home, especially when Samuel is away ministering to others. You have borne loneliness with amazing grace. Your home is a sanctuary for him because of your deep and selfless heart. Your value is like that of a pearl of great price.

May God protect you and may the Holy Spirit minister health, comfort, joy and peace to you in every way. May there never be a doubt that you are loved by the great God who created you and delights in you. You are his princess.

May your children grow in love with God because of your witness, and may they rise up and call you blessed.

I commit to pray for you in the days ahead. I commit to pray for your peace, safety and joy. May the Lord fulfill the secret dreams of your heart that He alone placed there.

The Word Given at the Dedication of Blessings Hope Healing Church January 2015

Remember your spiritual beginnings. Remember the day of your salvation and the price Jesus paid to make you God's children. Remember the miracles you have seen and experienced in this place. Remember that He overcame the grave for you and offers you His Holy Spirit to guide you, counsel you, and keep you close to His heart. Remember to share the Good News at every opportunity.

Retain your joy. Live in active, trusting peace in the shadow of the cross. Bless one another. Share with others the joy of your salvation and the hope of heaven, a hope that will not disappoint.

May the healing power of Jesus Christ flow freely in this church. May lives be made whole! May you reflect His sincere and unselfish love to all. May everyone who worships here be in awe of the Living God!

As you watch and wait for Christ's return, remember that the One who has made you whole will come back for you one of these fine days, and take you all to be with Him forever! Praise the Living God!

"May God himself, the God of peace, sanctify you through and through. May your whole spirit, soul and body be kept blameless at the coming of our Lord Jesus Christ. The one who calls you is faithful and he will do it." 1 Thessalonians 5:23-24

Key Scripture: *The Spirit of the Sovereign LORD is on me, because the LORD has anointed me to preach good news to the poor. He has sent me to bind up the brokenhearted, to proclaim freedom for the captives and release from darkness for the prisoner, to proclaim the year of the LORD'S favor and the day of vengeance of our God, to comfort all who mourn, and provide for those who grieve in Zion—to bestow on them a crown of beauty instead of ashes, the oil of gladness instead of mourning, and a garment of praise instead of a spirit of despair. They will be called oaks of righteousness, a planting of the LORD for the display of his splendor. Isaiah 61:1-3*

The Blessing Given at the Dedication of Samuel and Sharon's Home November 7, 2015

"By wisdom a house is built, and through understanding it is established; through knowledge its rooms are filled with rare and beautiful treasures." Proverbs 24:3-4

Samuel and Sharon, we now dedicate this home to be a place of peace and refuge for you and your family. May laughter flow through it easily and tears be wiped away. May visitors who enter drop their cares at Jesus' feet and accept His rest and peace. May they know that they can be themselves here because it is a home without hypocrisy or pretense or false pride. May they experience personally that Jesus heals the brokenhearted and sets the captive free. May they leave refreshed and with a clearer understanding of His great love for them. May compassion and constancy of faith crown you both to the glory of God.

Samuel, you have been through many fires in days past which have tested your faith. The opposition, adversity and danger revealed the purity of your love for the Lord whose Holy Spirit lives in you. Since you dared obey the dream God gave you to build Blessings Hope Educational Centre, evil came against you, but you never cursed the messenger or the thief or the disappointments or the hardships. You kept your eyes on Jesus and remembered His glory and goodness. You forgave, humbled yourself and began again. You continued loving and offering hope to those who had lost their way. Do not fear for He has given you the Kingdom.

Sharon, you share Samuel's hopes and dreams and childlike faith. You are not only God's friend, but Samuel's best friend and great love. You have faced your own trials and continued to trust God even when you were near death, and Jesus raised you up. You hold much wisdom in your heart and you can be trusted in all things.

You both are refueled by the gentleness and faithfulness of God. You are also refreshed by the carefree love of your children and those of Blessings Hope, and kept steady by their laughter and prayers.

So we dedicate this home to the glory of God. May safety and security guard its walls and angels stand watch over it. May dreams be born and nurtured here for generations to come. In Jesus' name, amen.

Message Given at Blessings Hope Educational Centre Graduation, November 2016

Blessings Hope Educational Centre was a dream born first in the heart of God. Then God planted it into the heart of a skinny young pastor who has a long history of dreaming big dreams for the children of Kenya. Then he shared it with us.

Dreaming with God and Pastor Samuel has become the most intense and beautiful faith walk of our lives. There are no promises other than the constancy of God's love and goodness.

Most amazing is that Blessings Hope's success is not because of money, property or programs. Nowhere in scripture does God anoint these things with his power. He anoints only people—ordinary people like you and me who are willing to have their hearts broken for what breaks his and who will hear and obey.

Think about it: When God wanted to deliver the children of Israel from bondage in Egypt, He anointed Moses, not a plan.

In the same way, God anointed David, not his sling, to kill the giant in the Valley of Elah. When he needed a wise judge and leader in Israel, he anointed Deborah, not the juniper tree under which she sat to judge issues among the people.

Likewise, God anointed Esther, not her beauty or courage, to speak for him to the king and save his people from extinction. And God anointed Peter at Pentecost, not his sermon, to turn the world upside down with the Gospel.

God still anoints men and women who honor and obey him.

He anoints men and women who, when treated unjustly, forgive— who love the unlovely and value a clean heart above all else.

He anoints those who rise early in the morning not for themselves, but for others.

Pastor Samuel has these qualities, and God has anointed him to lead this great endeavor. As a result, Blessings Hope is not just an excellent school. It is a home—a place where integrity, love and forgiveness flourish. It is a place of healing and great faith.

The teachers whom God has provided to guide your children also have these qualities. As with Samuel, the anointing is upon *them*, not the classrooms or the curriculum. Facilities and curricula are important, but they do not bear the anointing of God that changes lives. Men and women of grace and humility do.

Pastor Samuel and his wife Sharon, and the staff need you to hold them up to God every day. Thank God for them. Pray for their hearts to be always open to God's voice. Ask God to give them wisdom and to protect them from evil each day. Ask him to meet all their needs so they will be free from worry as they serve. Pray with me for them right now.

About Pastor Samuel Wafula

<p>astor Samuel W. Wafula is the founder and Director of Blessings Hope Educational Centre and Gospel Outreach Evangelistic Ministries (GOEM). He is also Presiding Bishop of New Covenant Bible Shalom Mission. God has blessed him and his beautiful wife Sharon Wamaitho with two children—Blessings Ellen and Nehemiah Strong Kibali.

HIs ministries are based in Kitale, Kenya, East Africa. By the grace of God, Pastor Samuel travels widely, serving as an international conference and crusade speaker. He has ministered across Kenya and in more than fifteen countries—Zimbabwe, Congo and South Africa, among others. His mission is found in the book of Isaiah 61:1, and it brings Samuel great joy to see God fulfilling His word in his life and ministry.

Pastor Samuel, Sharon, Nehemiah Strong and Blessings Ellen

How to Be Part of the Dream

Sponsor an orphan or teacher monthly or donate to one or more of the following:

- The High School and College Scholarship Fund
- The General Operations Fund
- The Emergency Fund for the security wall or the mini-bus

To donate or for more information about Blessings Hope Educational Centre and the Sponsorship Program, go to joycestrongministries.org

To invite Joyce to speak or share "The Dream" at your church, ministry, school or organization, contact her at: joycestrong@usa.net

More Books by Joyce Strong

Lambs on the Ledge

Seeing and Avoiding Danger in Spiritual Leadership

(In English, Russian and Kiswahili)

Caught in the Crossfire

Confronted by the Compassionate, Uncompromising Love of God

(In English and Russian)

Instruments for His Glory

Ministering in Harmony with God and Men

Leading with Passion and Grace

Encouraging and Mentoring Leaders in the Body of Christ

(In English, Russian and Kiswahili)

Journey to Joy

Discovering God's Love in Real Time

(In English, Russian and Kiswahili)

Of Dreams and Kings and Mystical Things:
A Novel on the Life of David

A Dragon, a Dreamer and the Promise Giver:
A Novel on the Life of King Solomon

True Love and the Dragon
A Novel of the Life of Mary Magdalene
(In English, Russian and Kiswahili)

24,000 copies of Joyce's books have been distributed freely throughout East Africa and Russia.